Praise for *The Wisdom of Your Face*

*"**The Wisdom of Your Face** brings the ancient art of Chinese face reading to life for modern Westerners. Jean Haner goes directly to the psychological and spiritual wisdom at its core. She guides us into a world where the lines of a face are no longer viewed as aesthetic problems to be erased but rather as the sacred calligraphy of an evolving soul. This is the product not only of a keenly perceptive and dedicated mind but also a deeply compassionate heart. It is a treasure trove of practical information and guidance, as well as poetry and magic that will be invaluable to anyone who is committed to helping themselves and others lead more authentic, meaningful, and rewarding lives."*

— **Lorie Dechar**, the author of *Five Spirits*

"Jean Haner reveals how to read a face like an open book. Her knowledge and insights show you how to interpret the life story written on every face, recognize the unique thoughts and feelings inscribed there, and truly understand all personality types. This book transforms the way you look into the mirror—and into the eyes of another person."

— **Terah Kathryn Collins**, the author of
The Western Guide to Feng Shui—Room by Room

ALSO BY JEAN HANER

The Wisdom of Your Child's Face: Discover Your Child's True Nature with Chinese Face Reading

Your Hidden Symmetry: How Your Birth Date Reveals the Plan for Your Life

THE
WISDOM
YOUR FACE
OF

THE WISDOM OF YOUR FACE

Change Your Life with Chinese Face Reading!

Jean Haner

HAY HOUSE, INC.

Carlsbad, California • New York City

London • Sydney • New Delhi

Published in the United States by: Hay House, Inc.: www.hayhouse.com
Published in Australia by: Hay House Australia Pty. Ltd.: www.hayhouse.com.au
Published in the United Kingdom by: Hay House UK, Ltd.: www.hayhouse.co.uk
Published in India by: Hay House Publishers India: www.hayhouse.co.in

Editorial supervision: Jill Kramer • *Design:* Tricia Breidenthal
Interior photos: Brian Hartman, Seattle, Washington

Portion of "Time Tested Beauty Tips" reprinted by permission of Sll/sterling Lord
Literistic, Inc., ©1973 by Sam Levenson

Library of Congress Cataloging-in-Publication Data

Haner, Jean.
  The wisdom of your face : change your life with Chinese face reading! / Jean Haner. -- 1st ed.
      p. cm.
  Includes bibliographical references.
  ISBN 978-1-4019-1755-5 (tradepaper)
  1. Physiognomy--China. I. Title.
  BF851.H28 2008
  138--dc22   2007023961

ISBN: 978-1-4019-1755-5

23 22 21 20 19 18 17 16 15 14
1st edition, February 2008

Printed in the United States of America

*For my
son, Jeffrey,
who opened
my heart.*

CONTENTS

PART III: LOOKING WITH LOVE

"For attractive lips, speak words of kindness.
For lovely eyes, seek out the good in people.
For a slim figure, share your food with the hungry.
For beautiful hair, let a child run
his fingers through it once a day.
For poise, walk with the knowledge
you'll never walk alone . . .
People, even more than things, have
to be restored, renewed, revived, reclaimed
and redeemed, redeemed and redeemed . . ."

— SAM LEVENSON

INTRODUCTION

Setting the Angel Free

You may know someone whom people just adore. Most likely this person isn't wrinkle free and doesn't have perfect features. Yet when he or she walks into the room, everyone's hearts just soar. What they're responding to is the information that radiates out from that individual's face, not physical appearance. When people are living according to their true nature, everyone finds them beautiful. When they're in balance with their own natural flow, their feelings aren't stifled or denied and they move through life with a joy and grace that's undeniably beautiful.

The astonishing secret is that your face can show you how to achieve this state for yourself. While you already know that your appearance can be changed in a negative way by stress in life, it also shows you the way *out* of an existence so affected by the challenges you encounter. Your face is a mirror of your inner blueprint, who you came here to be and what you came here to do.

We all have a unique inner design that has perfect coherence. The problem is that we don't get an owner's manual when we first arrive. So we rely to a great extent on the messages we get from family members, friends, the educational system, and our culture to figure out who we are and how we're supposed to think, feel, and behave. And of course, our natural ways of being and responding to life are soon reacted to by those around us.

Instead of being given guidance or support in allowing our true selves to be expressed and flourish, most of us grow up in a subtle atmosphere of judgment from others. We soon start believing there's something wrong with us. And what tends to happen is that we try to alter, limit, or even deny our real nature in order to find a way to be the person we think we're supposed to be. This puts us out of alignment, and soon we're living with imbalance and stress.

"I saw the angel in the marble and carved until I set him free," Michelangelo is reported to have said. He believed a sculpture already existed inside the stone, and he was simply freeing it by carving away what was *not* supposed to be there: "In every block of marble I see a statue as plain as though it stood before me, shaped and perfect in attitude and action. I have only to hew away the rough walls that imprison the lovely apparition to reveal it to the other eyes as mine see it."

A friend sent me those quotes after her experience in one of my face-reading workshops, saying that she saw my subject matter as very much the same thing. Learning to read your face can help you release what's not part of who you really are so that you can reveal the work of art within. The purpose of my work is to help you discover the hidden vitality and joy that is waiting for you so you can recover your original design and live according to its natural flow. In a world so focused on appearance, it seems to me that's the *best* way to look and feel beautiful!

I first discovered Chinese face reading in the late 1970s, when I married into a Chinese family and learned of it through my mother-in-law. I was attracted to studying it in order to understand my clients better. I wanted to use it to find ways to align myself with other people's energy, to see their needs more quickly and clearly so I could help them as effectively as possible. But it wasn't easy. Much of the information available about face reading was culturally inappropriate, judgmental, and negative. It has only been through 25 years

of study and experience—and the luck of finding some spectacular teachers along the way—that I bring this book to you now.

Face reading is based on the same ancient principles as Chinese medicine, and there are still doctors in China today who can diagnose illnesses simply by examining the face. But my work isn't for physical-health issues. The same qualities that reveal the state of your body also have parallels in your emotions. So the same aspects that a Chinese doctor would look at to evaluate your health can also be used to read your personality, and this is what my work is about. I use this knowledge to help people live according to their authentic nature, the unique emotional and energetic patterns that make them special in the world, so that *they* can be the ones who make everyone's hearts soar when they enter a room.

Every day I hear some version of *"That's me!"* in workshops and consultations. The astonishment shows as someone lights up with the epiphany that there's a reason why she's feeling the way she does, why her life experience has been what it has. This is what I hope that I can do for you.

In this book, we'll journey through the landscape of your face to discover the wisdom it has to offer you. Part I will provide the basic understanding of the origins of face reading and some of the ways it can be used. I'll explain how this information first began to "wiggle its hips" at me and why I find it so powerful. We'll see how important it is to make it meaningful and practical for our Western lives.

We'll cover the essential things to keep in mind while learning how to read a face. Then we'll start our travels by discovering what each decade, even each year of your life, has brought you. Seeing what your life experience has been to this point allows you to see how you may be creating your future based on your past. Just that knowledge alone can be incredibly powerful in helping you create a different life from here.

Part II is where you enter the most important stage of the journey. There, you'll explore the ancient foundation of Chinese face reading, the profound yet simple understanding that can change your life forever. I'll help you identify the five archetypes that are expressed in your face with your own unique design. You'll travel through all the features and markings your face has to offer,

learning the deeper truths each reveals about who you are and what you need to be happy.

Part III offers you additional ways to look at your face and gain even more insight about who is really there. You'll examine the different message each side of your face speaks, and what the horizontal zones have to offer as well. You'll end your journey with the opportunity to venture out on your own, trying out your new skills by practicing on some actual faces and then reading my interpretations afterward.

I often tell others that I'm one of the more skeptical people they'll ever meet. Even though I work in a field that many view as rather "woo-woo," I have a very active left brain and need to have things make rational sense before I can believe in them. It took a long time and a lot of study and practical application of the principles I now work with before I could fully believe they're valid.

And really, it's my clients and students who continue to prove to me that face reading works. It's the exhilarated confirmations I hear in workshops and consultations and the astonished e-mails I receive from people with amazing stories about how face reading proved true that continue to keep me in love with this work. They're what convinced me that its wisdom can forever change how you live your life. So I invite you to join me now in setting free that angel within.

Part 1

THE
MIRROR

"A man finds
room in the few square
inches of his face for the
traits of all his ancestors; for
the expression of all his
history, and his wants."

— RALPH WALDO EMERSON

Chapter 1

THE REFLECTION

How many faces have you gazed upon in your life? Each one you see is unique, belonging to that single human spirit alone. Most people assume they just have a combination of features, inherited through a mixture of genes from parents and ancestors, and with wrinkles developing due to aging. You might never imagine that each face holds deep truths about who that person is and why.

But what if you could tell just by looking at someone who he is inside—what his life has been like and how he will tend to think, feel, and behave? And what if you could see written on your own face the joy of the day you were married, the lessons learned in a difficult job, or the miraculous moment your child was born? Most important, what if the reflection in your mirror had a wealth of secrets to help reveal your inner spirit and how to allow its direct expression?

Many people think face reading must be a party trick, something to do with cosmetic surgery, or a way to categorize or manipulate people. It's actually based on the same ancient science as acupuncture and traditional Chinese medicine. References to this knowledge are found in texts dating back to 600 B.C.E., and its roots are said to be traced back to the period of the Yellow Emperor between 2697 and 2597 B.C.E. The original face readers were Taoist monks and scholars,

3

highly educated men whose role was said to have been a combination of priest, healer, and compassionate advisor.

Face reading was originally developed in association with the holistic belief that each part of the body is a representation of the entire body. Like a hologram where you shine a laser through one part of an image and create the entire picture, the face was considered a complete and perfect display of what was going on throughout the total physical self. The health of every major organ was believed to be mirrored by a different facial feature. In ancient China, doctors were not allowed to touch women to diagnose disease, so reading the face became an important technique.

These early physicians also recognized something that most of the West has only come to accept in the last few decades: The body and the mind exist in a circle of interaction. Chinese medicine perceived early on that emotions are an integral factor in health. The physical and mental selves are inseparable, and as such, the same information read on your face to investigate the condition of your body can also reveal the qualities of your inner emotional nature.

So while Chinese face reading can be used to evaluate your health, it also allows brilliant insights into the patterns of emotions you struggle with, your personal strengths and challenges, and even the people you'll be attracted to and the work you'll enjoy. Most important, face reading provides the answers to two essential questions for your life: *Who are you?* and *What is your calling?* And that is the focus of my work.

As I mentioned, my journey into this field began nearly 30 years ago when I married into a Chinese family. My very traditional mother-in-law helped my husband and me search for our first home, but she had some strange rules about what properties we could even look at. She didn't want us to consider a house at the end of a cul-de-sac, and refused to even think about looking at anything across the street from a cemetery. When we finally found a place she approved of, she was there 48 hours before we moved in, cleaning furiously—not just because of her high standards for cleanliness, but to scrub out all the leftover "energy" of the previous owners.

The rest of my husband's family was very embarrassed by all this and insisted she was just being superstitious. She believed in this strange thing that sounded like "fung sooey." This was long before feng shui, the ancient Chinese study of how our environment affects us, became popular in the West. But something about what she was saying intrigued me. She became the first of many feng-shui teachers I had over the following years, introducing me to the universal principles of balance that apply not only to our environment, but also to our health, our personalities, and all of life.

My mother-in-law also talked about face reading by noting "lucky" or "unlucky" features. Someone's nose showed she'd be bad luck to do business with; someone else's mouth revealed he'd be good luck as a husband. In fact, it was only years later that I learned of her disappointment with my own appearance—I didn't have the "moneybags" on my face that were a mark of luck for a wife! At that time, such beliefs seemed far too judgmental to me. I couldn't see the same intuitive logic behind it as I could with her pronouncements regarding real estate and the home, so I ignored it, thinking it was just folklore.

As feng shui become better known, I began teaching it and consulting all over the world, and this is what brought me back to Chinese face reading. In a feng-shui session, it was common to only have a couple of hours in which my clients expected me to change their lives! I would always have an in-depth conversation with people before even looking at their space in order to determine what challenges they might be struggling with and what their needs were at that point in time. But what would often happen is that the things they told me in our initial conversation were not really the important issues at hand. Often the deeper truths came up toward the end of our time together—if at all. So I was always searching for a way to read between the lines of what clients were telling me their problems were so that I could understand what was truly going on in their lives and how I could best help them.

I turned again to face reading and began to explore how the "good luck/bad luck" superstitions actually concealed some brilliant wisdom. This turned out to be what I needed in order to do powerful work with people, not only with feng shui, but soon as a tool of transformation all its own.

At first, I didn't share with my clients what their faces were revealing to me. I was simply using the information to determine

how I could do the most effective feng-shui work for them. And it certainly gave us exciting results—amazing changes were taking place.

But soon I just couldn't hold back, and I began to share what I was seeing on their faces. And what had started out as just a half-hour conversation on the couch was turning into a couple of hours of transformational work. More than one person said to me: "You know, I feel like *I've* been feng-shuied. I don't even care about what to do with the house!"

A beautiful thing was happening: As each client and I sat together in our consultation, the true essence of this lovely being was revealed. She could see herself for who she was—not in the light of judgment that she was so used to, but as natural and right. It was exhilarating for both of us to see how the wisdom read on her face really seemed to give her permission to finally live in alignment with her original self. Once she saw who she really was, then she could discover how to move into her true calling, based on what the features of her face told us.

Discovering Ourselves

One of the first times this kind of revelation happened for me was both poignant and amusing. I was asked to feng-shui an apartment for a woman who worked as a bookkeeper. She'd been in that position for ten years, but in fact her heart's desire was to be a firefighter. She'd trained intensely, and every year for seven years had taken the very strenuous physical test to get her dream job. But every year for seven years, she'd failed miserably. As a last resort, she thought perhaps there might be something in the energy of her home environment that was preventing her from accomplishing her goal. Maybe feng-shuiing her home would allow her to finally pass the test.

The first thing I saw when I stepped through her front door was a glossy wall calendar with a photo of a bare-chested firefighter in a sexy pose. And throughout the space there were pictures of fire engines and people dressed up in all the gear—she certainly was

focused on the subject! There was even a portrait of a firefighter beside her bed, the first thing she saw when she woke up in the morning.

But when we sat down on the couch together and I turned to study her face, my heart sank. Nowhere in her features did I see anything that said "firefighter" to me. Instead, what I saw was all about love and relationships. Rather than dashing around town combatting blazes, a strong need for an intimate partnership and family life was written there.

I tactfully tried to explain that I didn't think feng shui could help her with her goal. As delicately as possible, I described what her face was telling me, hoping that she wouldn't be too disappointed. For some time my client stared at me with a blank expression. But then she brightened and held up her hand. "I think I get it!" she exclaimed. "I don't want to *be* a firefighter—I want to *have* one!" And she proceeded to get a firefighter boyfriend and is now happily married to him, although she's still working as a bookkeeper to this day. She wasn't wrong—she did need firefighter energy in her life. She was just misinterpreting the message of how it needed to appear.

If you're like many of us, you've spent years trying to feel comfortable in your own skin and to figure out what you should do with your life. This is your most important purpose: to fully move into the power of your authentic self and to discover how to put that power to work in the world. There's a reason why you are here and a special way to accomplish your role in the world. But so many of us feel a lack of clarity around all this. We feel out of touch with our true nature and aren't sure why.

I have a theory that we tend to go through life blaming ourselves for being who we are. We think we're doing something wrong, and if only we could fix it, we'd finally be okay. But that's really like blaming ourselves for having short legs or curly hair. It's just who we are, our inner blueprint, our personal software.

We're all born with a unique set of strengths and challenges—individual tendencies to think, feel, and behave in special ways. There really is an underlying coherence to every person's inherent energy that makes sense and has meaning. But we've been taught for most of our lives to try to fit into someone else's pattern! We grow up immersed in our family's judgments and expectations about who we are and who they want us to be. We're all affected by the constant messages our culture imposes on us, as well as our early experiences in school and in society as a whole. By the time we're adults, our true selves are often lost in the layers of the influences of others. We've identified with all this information and no longer feel that inner balance. Their judgment of us has seamlessly become our own self-judgment. Our true nature is a mere whisper in the cacophony of voices in our heads.

So much of the stress you hold and the ways you keep yourself stuck have to do with how far you've traveled from your original self. You can release that tension by identifying who's actually there under all those layers and why that pure essence is really perfect as it is. And when you let go of that stress . . . when you can stop blaming yourself for being who you are, it frees up an enormous amount of energy to move forward in life. When you can embrace your true nature, you finally get out of your own way. You can actually be yourself—on purpose.

I had one client whose face made it obvious to me that for him to feel happy in life, he needed to be in the public eye, ideally at the center of a wide and strong network of connections. He showed huge potential for being a powerful teacher, authority figure, or even performer. However, this man had grown up in a family that judged anyone in the spotlight as vain and egotistical. He was criticized for his charismatic personality as being self-centered and wanting all the attention. He eventually chose a career as a health-care practitioner, humbly working behind the scenes with individual clients.

But even though he was good at his work, he felt very unsatisfied and eventually became depressed and was often ill, succumbing to every virus that came his way. Similarly, suppression of your original nature will of course lead to unhappiness over time; and in the long run, this kind of denial of your power can contribute to physical imbalance in your life, too.

As my client and I worked together, I could see the weight lifting from his shoulders as I reflected back to him the inner spirit that I saw. His relief was palpable as he saw himself in an entirely new and positive light, one that embraced all kinds of possibilities for living out who he really was. As a result, he's now an active teacher in his field, making speeches at national conferences and leading a professional organization in a way that uses the best of all his talents.

Chinese face reading gives you a way to recognize who you really are, just as this man did, and to reach a compassionate place of understanding for yourself. It can free you from living in reaction or responsibility to what others think. Instead, you can move forward with a spacious new awareness of your calling in the world, based on living in harmony with your original nature.

Understanding Others

Once a woman came to me with a photograph of her new boyfriend. Although they had great chemistry, there were some warning bells going off for her that she wanted checked out. She said that he seemed to have a tendency to be needy and didn't respect her boundaries: "It's like he wants to be attached at the hip!" Whenever she wanted some time alone, he insisted that he loved her so much that he couldn't go home but would be happy to just sit quietly and not bother her. This drove her crazy, as she was the kind of person who needed her space. She was worried that this was just a portent of things to come—that he would be too clingy and possibly too demanding or controlling.

The moment I looked at his picture, I saw from his particular combination of eyes, cheeks, and mouth that he was the kind of person who really loved being in a relationship and would want to lavish nonstop affection on his partner. In fact, the idea of being alone was the antithesis of happiness to him, so he wouldn't be likely to understand her need for solitude.

It wasn't that they couldn't have a wonderful relationship together; it was simply a matter of awareness. It was actually an enormous relief for her to understand that this wasn't an issue of control or domination. When she understood that his behavior

was due to his natural desire for closeness, she saw different ways in which she could communicate with him when this subject came up. Since we also discussed what her face showed as her own contribution to the situation, she realized what a gift his stable, caring nature was for her.

So once you can stop blaming yourself for being who you are, something even more amazing can happen: You stop blaming other people for being who *they* are as well! The impact on relationships can be huge. When you can see from your husband's eyebrows that he really *does* have to play basketball twice a week, it can be a tipping point in your marriage. When you can know by looking at your client's mouth that you need to ask to see the family photos before getting down to business, it creates the space for immediate compatibility and successful communication. And when your own cheeks explain why a picture hanging slightly crooked on the wall will drive you crazy unless you can straighten it, you can begin to create a new perspective on your own life.

Your face is really a mirror of who you are inside. It reveals the essence of your original nature and what you need to feel in balance. It shows you the special talents, skills, and abilities you have most strongly and what your challenging qualities are as well. Knowing how to read this information opens a way for you to live your life in alignment with your own natural flow, find the life path that gives you joy, seek out relationships that nurture you, and most of all, create a place for you to live in compassion for yourself and others.

Who are you? What is your calling? As you'll soon see, you already have everything you need to find out.

Nourishing What Manifests

In my work with feng shui, I had the good fortune to study with a second-generation practitioner, a man who was also an acclaimed qi gong master and in such demand that he traveled back to Beijing several times a year to teach there, in addition to his practice in the U.S. His family, deeply involved in Taoism, had been forced to

flee China for Taiwan in the 1949 civil war. He would sometimes tell stories of his uncles, Taoist monks, who would levitate in their chairs!

Because he couldn't drive and needed rides to his feng-shui consultations, I was his happy volunteer chauffeur. There's no better way to learn something than to observe an expert in action. I admired his genius at simplifying feng shui to its essence and producing recommendations for his clients that were amazingly simple but precisely attuned to their needs. He always found the few perfect things that would tip everything back into balance, like a master acupuncturist knowing exactly the one right needle to use.

One of the things he told me is something I recall each time I work: "Watch what naturally manifests." He taught that we don't need to try to figure out how to "fix" something or analyze it endlessly to know the right thing to do. Instead, always see what is trying to emerge in any situation and support that which is already showing up, rather than trying to force something that's against the grain, not in alignment with the natural flow.

I found this profoundly meaningful in face reading. I believe we're all always trying to "naturally manifest" the special energy we are. But early on in life, we learn that we have to stifle and deny it, try to make it match what others think it should be, and what we believe will finally allow us to have the life we desire. Instead, that energy should be nourished, supported, and allowed to flourish in its full glory. This is the beautiful gift face reading gives us. It allows us to see and recognize who we are, what we need, and how we can be loved and loving in the world.

Chapter 2

TRANSLATING
THE WISDOM

Your face is a product of your genetics, your environment, and your life experiences. It shows who you are, where you've been, and where you're going; it reveals your unique potential and what you need to feel happy. The information in your features can be a wonderful resource to help you create a life that's truly meaningful and fulfilling. All you have to do is look in the mirror.

In fact, you don't need to know anything special in order to get information from looking at someone. We all unconsciously read and react to faces throughout the day. There are 100 billion nerve cells in the cortex, almost the entire back half of the brain. Most of these are devoted primarily to seeing; and of those, a large percentage is dedicated only to recognizing faces.

Research shows how important faces are to human beings. According to a study in the journal *Pediatrics*, babies only nine minutes old already naturally prefer to look at pictures of faces over any other pictures. Amazingly, at 12 hours after birth, an infant prefers her mother's photo over that of another mother. I've even heard of a software program in which the password isn't a series of letters or numbers, but rather a certain pattern of faces. It's been found that while people tend to forget regular passwords, they won't forget a sequence of humans!

A recent study reported that women can identify which men like children just by looking at their faces. Photographs were shown to the test subjects and they were asked to select the individuals whom they believed enjoyed kids. The women were nearly 70 percent accurate, both with the men who liked children and those who specifically said they didn't.

We even respond to how wide or narrow someone's face is. Psychological studies show that people with broad faces are considered more trustworthy and friendly. The theory is simply that when you think you can see more of someone's face, you subconsciously feel as if that person isn't hiding anything.

Important information can be read even in fleeting expressions. This was an integral part of Dr. John Gottman's work at the University of Washington that revolutionized the understanding of intimate relationships. In his fascinating research, he developed a system that could predict with incredible accuracy whether a marriage would end in divorce.

Early in his studies, he filmed couples having conversations, but he turned off the sound and only watched the expressions on their faces as they spoke to each other. He found that repeated looks of contempt and disgust were major predictors of divorce. So much can be read just from the brief emotions that flicker across someone's face in any moment. Interestingly, it was also discovered that these same expressions were indicators of a high level of contagious diseases among the test subjects, and possibly long-term illnesses.

There was even a 40-year study that showed that people's smiles in their college graduation pictures predicted their levels of happiness for the rest of their lives! The subjects were interviewed at regular intervals over the years, and it was discovered that the intensity of their grins at age 21 foretold their future life experiences. If two major muscle actions were present (in the zygomatic major muscle around their mouths and the orbicularis oculi muscle around their eyes), the smiles were genuine; and those individuals consistently reported having happy lives. It's doubtful they had smooth sailing all that time—they may have had divorces, been ill, or lost jobs, just like all of us. Rather, it seems to have been their attitude toward

life that determined how they judged their experiences.

Those people who weren't smiling in their graduation pictures, or who showed false smiles without both those muscle actions present, gave very different reports. They said their lives hadn't been happy overall. They probably had the same percentage of difficult times, but the subtle signs on their faces at the age of 21 showed how they were already predisposed toward negative attitudes.

You see, your face holds so many clues to who you are inside. It's really a map of your inner territory—your strengths, your challenges, and the patterns of emotion and behavior you're carrying that will continue to define your life experience. You may have heard the saying: "If you keep on doing what you've always done, you'll keep on getting what you've always gotten." If you can become aware of how you're building your future based on your past, you'll gain the power to change from that moment forward. This is another of the opportunities face reading provides you.

Judgment

Sometimes when people hear that I teach face reading, they exclaim, "Oh, I already read faces all the time." As we've seen above, it *is* true that we all naturally observe and react to those around us. But when most people "read" others, it's not with any real understanding of what they're seeing. Rather, it's usually a combination of judgment and intuition. One way we tend to react is with an unconscious memory based on our past experiences, which leads to judgment. Someone's eyes or facial structure may subtly remind us of a person with whom we had a positive or negative experience. This can color our subconscious reaction to this new acquaintance in ways that may not be helpful or meaningful in our present situation. A woman in one of my workshops suddenly realized that she'd chosen a certain karate teacher for her son because his face reminded her of a favorite uncle. But her son found the instructor's teasing personality discouraging. She realized that her personal history was intruding on her ability to accept that it wasn't a good match.

There's a second way in which unconscious judgment affects our reactions to others: Whether we're aware of it or not, we're all reading each other's energy as we interact. If people are at a frequency that resonates with ours, we usually feel an affinity for them. If they're at a different frequency, we may not feel much of a connection, or we may even have an aversion to them. But these conclusions may not be valid for the purpose at hand. Having the awareness about why we're responding to someone as we are empowers us to make knowledgeable choices rather than being lost in reaction. Face reading teaches how to perceive this energy in a conscious way.

Another student in one of my workshops realized that this had happened with her son's third-grade teacher. She'd nearly transferred him out of this woman's class because she felt the teacher was far too nervous and high-strung. She seemed to harp on every detail and never let anything slide. This mother had a more laid-back personality and would become stressed every time she had to communicate with her. But it was this teacher who spotted her son's learning disability after it had been missed the three previous years. The mother realized that it was because of this finely tuned awareness that the problem had been discovered. Her son may have been saved years of frustration in school because of the person whose energy set her on edge.

After attending my class, she told me that she now had the tools to approach her son's teacher in a way that eliminated the tense reaction to her personality. And she also understood how to talk to the woman, what words to use, and even how to hold her body and how far away to stand so that the teacher wouldn't close her out because of her own reaction to the mother's energy. My student said it was like she'd discovered that she could suddenly speak a foreign language.

Intuition

We also use our intuition when we look at people, which *can* be incredibly useful. This is that feeling of "knowing before we know," having the answer to a question before we even begin to think it through. Intuition has been greatly undervalued in Western culture, but fortunately times are changing. However, most of us can't always summon that gut feeling when it's needed.

For many people, without training, practice, or awareness, it's rarely possible to discern whether reactions are based on unconscious judgment or true intuitive knowing. But when you come into balance within yourself, you're more easily aware of when your personal biases are intruding, and your inner guidance can flow without resistance.

You can use face reading to validate what your intuition is saying to you. I've received so many e-mails about this after workshops that I really think face reading could be a whole new way of training your instincts. One student who's a personal coach recently wrote that he'd felt like he was beating his head against a brick wall when it came to working with a certain man. The client had landed a job that put him in charge of long-term planning for a large corporation. The coach had created a beautifully organized system to help him achieve his goals in this new position and worked hard to keep him on track, but he couldn't stick with the plan and seemed to be becoming increasingly unhappy in his job.

After attending my session, the coach realized that a gut feeling had been nagging at him all this time, but he'd been ignoring it. "Since day one with this man, I had a strong sense that this job just wasn't him. After the face-reading workshop, it only took a single look at my client's face to get confirmation that he was probably heading down the wrong career path entirely." His face showed he was never going to excel in handling complex projects; and in fact, long-term planning was certainly not his forte. Instead, he'd thrive in a competitive position that provided short-term challenges and few requirements to create complicated strategies. With this insight, the coach had a renewed vision for ways to help him gain success and satisfaction in his work.

Another student e-mailed to tell me that she's been practicing her face reading "backward" in her dating life. "I get my intuitive hits and *then* check his face for proof. So far, it's worked every time, and I'm sure it's already saved me some heartache!"

THE WISDOM OF YOUR FACE

Learning what your own and others' faces really have to say can be an incredibly empowering experience as you gain a new understanding of the reactions you've had to people in the past. This can sometimes confirm what you sensed and validate your intuition, or it can show you that you were bringing too much of your personal judgment into the situation. And because learning what your own face has to tell you also helps you come into balance, you can move through life from here with your intuitive intelligence at the ready.

Four Means Four

In my work with feng shui, I soon came to see that the ideas need translation for it to be useful in our Western lives. The discipline evolved over thousands of years in China, and much of it is meaningful only within that culture. In order for it to be applicable in this part of the world, I needed to be aware of what aspects weren't culturally appropriate and might need interpretation.

For instance, a very simple example is the issue of the number four. In Chinese, the word for this number sounds like the word for *death,* so it's considered very unlucky to have the numeral in your life. No one wants a four in his house address, license plate, or cell-phone number. However, in the West, the number four means . . . four. There's no connotation of misfortune, and even the concept of "luck" doesn't have as much significance in most North American or European countries. Yet I saw Western feng-shui consultants advising people to go through the legal acrobatics to change their house number because it had a four in it!

In many Asian cultures, the color white is associated with mourning and death. However, in the West, it tends to connote purity and cleanliness. Even the so-called lucky directions in feng shui have a lot to do with the country the concepts originated in. One reason why south is considered beneficial in China is because in many parts of the country, if your house faces south you don't have dust storms from the Gobi Desert blowing in your front door! Historically, the direction had a positive meaning as well: China was conquered by armies moving down from the north, so facing south has long been linked to a national sense of success. These associations don't necessarily translate to other regions of the world.

Similarly, when I began my study of face reading, I soon saw that cultural influences would need to be considered there as well. The traditional Chinese approach was all about judgment; everything was either good luck or bad luck, usually based on issues of money or materialism. If a feature was lucky, it usually meant it would help you get financial or business success.

Further, the proclamations of what was fortunate seemed in many cases to be stuck in an entirely different era. Take the attribute called "Bossy Woman Cheeks." It's supposed to be very unlucky to marry a woman with this kind of prominent feature because she'll try to run your life! Perhaps 3,000 years ago in China, it was indeed unlucky to have a wife like this, or to be a woman with cheeks that showed you wanted some say in things. But in this day and age, this quality might be considered a positive, a sign of power. If you have the ability to speak up and state what you want, that means you're a strong woman. And in our times, women in most careers need to have the ability to hold authority in everything from running a household to managing a business.

Traditionally, a man with a full mouth was considered to be destined to die in ruin. This feature was considered to be a sign he was lascivious and prone to affairs, so he'd spend all of his money and energy on women, dying worn-out and destitute. Well, that's one way of interpreting what a full mouth means. It is indeed a sign of someone who's generous, who knows how to enjoy life, and for whom relationships are very important. This could easily be a man with many friends, who has many ways of enjoying the pleasures in life, and who's emotionally available in relationships. Sounds like a catch!

So for me, it was important to replace the judgment with awareness. It's not about what's right or wrong with you, but simply about understanding the essence of who you are and how you can most easily live in balance with your natural flow. A woman with "power" cheeks probably wouldn't feel satisfied in a subservient

position at work; a man with a full mouth wouldn't be happy without fulfilling personal relationships.

As I mentioned, face reading originally developed in China thousands of years ago as a method of health diagnosis. As its power became better understood, its influence soon spread beyond medicine, and it was used for important life decisions such as matchmaking and choosing whom to do business with. But over time, this knowledge, much like feng shui, gradually degenerated into superstition among the general population. Stripped of the rich philosophy of its Taoist origins, what was left was just lots of rules without any understanding about the principles behind them.

So in much of the culture, the practice lost its depth and became quite fatalistic. Your face determined your destiny. If you were born with "unlucky" features, that was pretty much it for you! Of course this is far too limiting a viewpoint, not useful or meaningful in ancient China, let alone in our current life and times. To assume there are "bad" and "good" features reduces the wisdom to a set of fear-based proclamations that don't help anyone.

Additionally, your face is only a reflection of who you are inside at any one point in time. As you change, so does your appearance. Your future is written in your features only insofar as they're a mirror of who you've been up until this point. As you transform inside, your future shifts. It isn't predetermined.

There's a wonderful quote attributed to the Buddha: "What you are is what you have been, what you will be is what you do now." Your face shows who you've been in the past and how that's contributing to the person you're becoming. And in every moment, you always have the power to change.

Your face reflects every adjustment you make. I've witnessed dramatic physical changes after people have experienced personal growth and transformation. I've seen eyebrows grow in differently, lips change, and wrinkles diminish or disappear. At times, even complexion, cartilage, and bone structure appear altered as a result of real inner work. Your face seems to truly be a mirror of who you are inside.

As You Use This Book

Here's an important note as you continue to go through this book: If you're using this information to read what your own face has to say about yourself, try to start out with an empty mind. Look in the mirror as if you'd never seen this individual before. By this point in life, you're probably the last person who can look at your own face objectively. You were teased about your nose as a child, you're self-conscious about your ears, or you're worried you'll end up with wrinkles just like your mother's. So it can be very difficult to see what's really there.

It may be helpful to use this book with a couple of friends who can offer their own observations about what they see in your features. And it's also useful to have other faces to compare your own to. In my workshops, we always have practice sessions in groups for this very reason. Getting insights from more than one person and being able to compare yourself to others is a great way to see "what's in front of your nose!"

As you start to look at individual features, you should judge their size by comparing them to the scale of the rest of the parts of that particular face. A large chin on one person may look small on another. Additionally, always read within races—that is, compare Caucasian faces to other Caucasians, African to African, Asian to Asian, and so on. You can read mixed-race faces, too; it just takes a little more practice.

It's also essential to keep in mind that there is no cookie-cutter approach. The meaning of one feature is often modified or even controlled by the meaning of others. As you read this book, you may find yourself thinking, *Oh no! I've got that kind of nose! . . .* or ear, or mouth, and so on. The essential thing to keep in mind is that all your features dance together to create the unique choreography that is you and only you. Some diminish the effect of others; some emphasize them. It's the beautiful, intricate design of nature; and it's what makes you like nothing else in the universe . . . yet like everything else.

Chapter 3

MAPPING
YOUR JOURNEY

One of the easiest ways to begin exploring your face is to learn how to observe the road map of your journey through life—how each decade or even individual years have been or will be—based on who you are at this point in time.

Each major feature stands for approximately one decade of your life. A large, strong, or especially beautiful feature is considered to mean that these years will be positive overall. In addition, the parts foretell your general pattern of experience through life.

The two most important kinds of features on your face are called "Mountains" and "Rivers." The Mountains are bony: forehead, nose, chin, and jaw. Rivers are the soft areas that have some kind of moisture: ears, hairline, eyes, and mouth.

In general, the Mountains are considered to be times in life when you are developing your "yang" energy—you're out in the world more, having experiences and accomplishing things. The Rivers are when you move into the more "yin" stages of your life, often when deep emotional issues emerge to be worked on. These tend to be times when you encounter challenging relationships or go through the process of inner growth in some way.

Let's go through this topography in order to see how it can show you the big picture of the stages of your life.

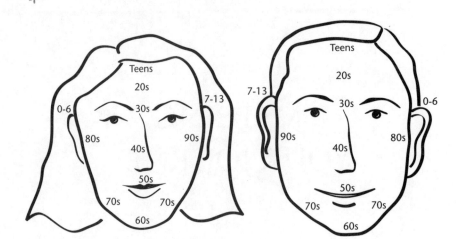

Fig. 1: The Decades of Life

Ears = Childhood

One of the many things you can read in your ears is your child-hood experience from conception through age 13. For women, the right ear shows the period of time from conception through age 6, and the left ear from ages 7 through 13. For men, it's the opposite: The left ear shows conception through age 6, and the right ear 7 through 13 (see Fig. 2 on page 26).

This is the very beginning of your experience of life, when you arrive vulnerable, innocent, and unable to protect yourself emo-tionally or physically. So any significant difficulties in childhood can be especially powerful in forming who you are; they can rever-berate throughout the rest of your life. If a challenge experienced at this time does have a lifelong influence on you, it can mark your ears. A visible effect on the ear can indicate a range of experience from merely a sign of general stress or a time of emotional upset, to trauma or even abuse at that point in life. Usually, the stronger and more noticeable the marking, the stronger the distress involved in the experience at that time.

To begin, feel the point at the upper part of your ear where it attaches to the side of your head. Women, check this on your right ear, men, on your left. This spot can show you if there was any experience between conception and birth that is currently affecting your life. It's believed that the months you spend in utero are an important influence on your emotional development. If something happens to stress you in your prebirth or birth experience, it can leave a mark on your ear at this point. In most cases, this spot won't feel remarkable. However, if you feel a dip, hole, or bump or see a discoloration or anything unusual at this spot, it could mean something significant happened during that early time in your life. It may be interesting to look at the ears of some friends to get experience in how different this part of the body can be!

It may be hard to believe that you could have a prebirth experience that could really have much of an impact on you, but recent scientific discoveries indicate that this is entirely possible. Neuropeptides, the "molecules of emotion" that neuroscientist Candace Pert's groundbreaking work studied, carry the messages of feelings from the brain throughout the body, creating actual physical changes. It's now known that the mother's neuropeptides cross the placenta and enter the baby's bloodstream; emotional trauma for Mom can cause fetal distress. In an Italian study in the 1990s, researchers asked a group of pregnant women and their husbands to briefly simulate an argument. Even though the parents were just playacting, the fetuses went into distress inside their mothers' bodies.

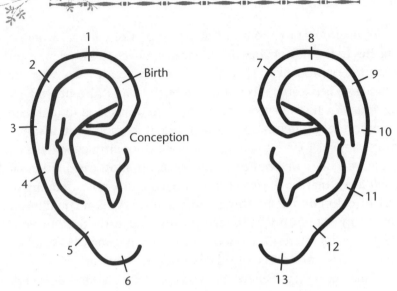

Fig. 2: For women, the right ear shows life experience from conception through age six. The left ear reveals ages 7 through 13. For men, begin with the left ear first, then the right.

It's important to note that your mother could have had stress during pregnancy (whose didn't?) or you could have had a very traumatic birth, but if that experience is not still impacting your life in some way, you won't find any indication of it at the ear. You'll only carry indications of issues that are currently influences in your life. A marking can mean that the stress is still an obstacle in your path. However, it may also mean that the experience was a powerful lesson that has been integrated, and the sign remains to show how important it was. You'll know which is true for you.

So if you see a marking or feel any dip or bump at this point, it's an indication that, in some way, your experience at that early stage is a significant factor in who you are at this point in time. But this doesn't mean you should be concerned if you find something unusual. This is just one portion of your story, a small part of what makes up the unique individual you are. You're just beginning your journey of exploration with your face!

To read the rest of the story of childhood, look for any significant changes to the rim (the helix) of your ears. As you can see in

Figure 2, each year of childhood is approximately another half inch along the rim. If there's an area where the rim becomes thin (Fig. 3), this often indicates a time during which you felt a lack of safety or something was taken away. For instance, when the edge thins out at the top of the ear, it means that this occurred soon after birth. In these cases, I often find that there was a parent's absence, such as an illness of the mother where she was separated from her baby at this time. There could have been a divorce at this point in the child's life, and one parent moved away, or something less dramatic but still stressful.

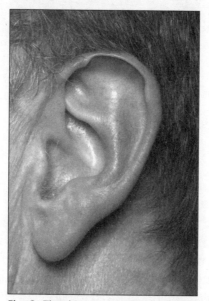

Fig. 3: The thin area on the rim of this ear represents a time when a sense of safety and support was missing, starting at around age one and lasting for about two years.

The length of the thin area of the rim indicates how long the stress lasted. If there's only a short area that has thinned, this means the influence of the event or experience lasted for a short amount of time. It could reflect the birth of a sibling, when attention was taken away from you; it might be the age when you began school or

the family pet died. It's important to recognize that it's not so much *what* happens to you in life, but how you *feel* about the event.

If the rim shows a notch (Fig. 4), this was an individual incident, some stressful one-time event. This can mark something physical such as an accident or illness.

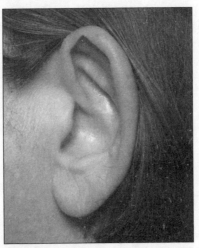

Fig 4: The notch at the top of this ear shows a single stressful incident around the age of eight.

If the rim of the ear is pressed down, or pinched flat almost as if it had been ironed, this is a sign of suppression during that stage of life. For instance, there was a student in one of my workshops who grew up with parents who were religious fundamentalists. She was homeschooled and not allowed to play with children outside of her church. Her parents were very strict in their beliefs and severe with punishment with respect to any violation of their rules. She said that for her entire childhood she was oppressed and controlled, and both her ears showed this pressed-down rim. At age 16, she fled home and never returned.

A bumpy area on the rim of the ear (Fig. 5) indicates a time of ups and downs in that period of childhood. However, if there is a big protrusion, this is actually considered to be a positive. The Chinese believe that anything that sticks out on the face is beneficial. This can mean the experience at that age was pleasant, although not necessarily. I've found in my work that the person with this pattern sometimes reports that what happened was difficult at the time, but it actually turned out to have a strongly positive influence in the long run.

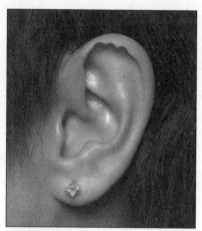

Fig. 5: The bumpy area at the top of this ear reflects a period of ups and downs in life at about age eight or nine.

Although a marking on the ear can exist exactly in the spot that corresponds with the age at which the event happened, it's also possible for it to be approximate. A general rule is that it may have happened one year before or after the date indicated. This can also be because the stress caused by the event may have had its strongest effect in the period following it. For example, if your twin brothers were born when you were three, the stress of not getting enough attention from your parents may have been felt in the following year or two. It's important to keep this in mind as you're reading your ear or someone else's.

Any marking, indentation, scar, wrinkle, spot, or discoloration on the ear has meaning. But you can get a bit too neurotic about examining each and every tiny dot anywhere on your face! What matter most are the easily observable, most prominent things. I also place a lot of importance on looking at what your ear shows about your first three years, as we know that in many ways, those early years set up your expectations, your belief systems for the rest of your life.

However, if you see someone with an ear that looks severely mangled or disfigured at any point, have great compassion for them because it's most likely a sign of childhood abuse. To be clear, this doesn't mean that their ears were actually damaged. The experience of severe distress in childhood will mark this body part, whether it's due to emotional difficulty, illness, or physical injury anywhere on the body.

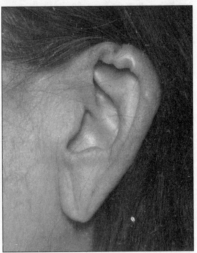

Fig. 6: This marking shows a sign of more severe stress around age eight.

I once had a client with an extremely disfigured right ear, with the strongest marking where events from the age of nine would be indicated. I'd worked with this man for some time, so I was able to get a good feel for his overall life experience. When I asked what happened to him around the time he was nine years old, I wasn't surprised by his answer. He looked astonished, and confided that he'd been sexually abused by an uncle he'd dearly trusted. But what was most saddening for me was to observe the issues he'd been struggling with in his adult life. He reported the same experiences over and over with similar language: He formed a deep friendship but it broke apart because he was "betrayed and abused"; a business partner had "tricked and cheated" him; a spiritual teacher had "used and betrayed" him. He was suspicious of everyone by this point in time. It seemed as if his current experiences were the emotions of his childhood trauma being played out again and again.

However, the fact that this could possibly show on his ear as an indication of a lifelong pattern finally led him to consider counseling for the first time, doing the inner work that would free him from repeating the past. I saw him again after several years of personal growth, and the rim of his right ear, while not completely normal, had changed—a reflection of his true personal transformation.

A man who came to one of my face-reading workshops was missing the entire earlobe on his right ear, and had been born that way. When we discussed what had happened to him when he was 13, he said, "That was when my whole life changed." It turned out that he'd been the victim of a horrendous prank by his class at school and was publicly humiliated in a terrible way. This cruel trauma resulted in a severe phobia that completely altered his existence from that point on. Even as an adult, he avoided social events, couldn't go on business trips, and worked at home alone as much as possible.

It's important to note that he was born with his ear disfigured this way, *before* he had the traumatic experience. Markings can show up before or after stress. If it had been spotted before that age was reached, then support could have been prepared for him, to at least help him better survive the situation. And in rare cases such as this one, I might have even recommended plastic surgery to repair the abnormality. When I've seen this done in the past, there has still been a slight stress but nothing as extreme as described above.

Hairline = Adolescence

Your hairline represents your experience in adolescence, a time when you're dealing with the next stage in your emotional development. You've gained more ability to deal with challenges, so stress during these years will be experienced differently from that of childhood. Yet you're still not emotionally mature, and as we all know, the result is that adolescence can bring plenty of difficult times! Any

upsets in this phase of life will affect the shape of your hairline. If yours is irregular—in other words, if it has a lot of ups and downs rather than being a smooth shape such as a straight line or oval—your teen years were probably especially challenging (Fig. 7).

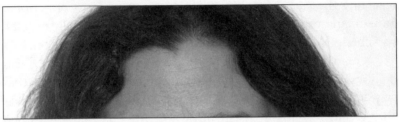

Fig. 7: This hairline is slightly irregular, meaning adolescence wasn't an easy experience.

Forehead = 20s

Your forehead shows your life experiences as you move into and through the decade of your 20s. Your upper forehead shows your late teens, the middle of your forehead shows your early through mid-20s, and the lower forehead represents what you went through in your late 20s.

The forehead is one of the Mountains on the face—a yang, active time, when most people go out into the world for the first time. If you've gone through this period, you know how it is to be at the brink of this decade, just coming out of adolescence and so sure that you know what the world is all about. But then you go out and begin to experience what life is *really* like—and you have a lot of surprises!

When you're surprised, what facial expression do you make? You raise your eyebrows, creating temporary horizontal wrinkles on your forehead. With many unexpected events during your 20s, it's no wonder that wrinkles on the face often begin to form on the forehead first (Fig. 8).

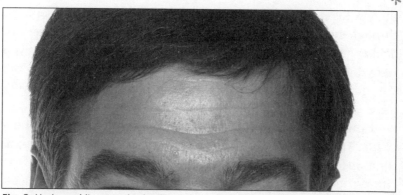

Fig. 8: Horizontal lines on the forehead show the strong experiences of the late teens and the 20s.

A colleague of mine left home at 19 and traveled the world in his 20s, enduring many rough experiences in developing countries but learning an enormous amount about himself and life in general. His forehead was one of the most deeply marked I've ever seen, a series of carved horizontal lines set closely together, revealing the adventures he'd had but also how much he'd learned! These kinds of creases are only indicators of the intensity of experience at that stage of life. They don't mean someone has done anything wrong or is troubled; instead, they can show life lessons that were well learned.

If you have horizontal lines on your forehead, therefore, this means that you had some powerful experiences in your 20s. In examining any of these furrows more closely, you want to look for ones that are continuous and unbroken. If a line isn't complete, but has a break and then continues later across the forehead, this is a sign of an experience in the 20s that resulted in a lesson not completely understood. This merely means that life will probably continue to give you opportunities to work through the issue.

Eyes = 30s

You can read the experiences of the decade of your 30s by looking at the area of your face around your eyes. The eyes are one of the yin River features, and this is often a period when people go through emotional "stuff," whether in relationships or careers, or deliberately pursue personal-growth work. Issues you thought you were done with may reemerge to be dealt with on a deeper level. You may start to question things about your life again, or you'll have experiences that force you to do so.

However, it's appropriate and healthy work to do at this time of life. This is often when you make your first real strides in personal growth—sometimes unwillingly. It seems as though you either choose to do so, or it's thrust upon you through a difficult relationship with a partner, child, parent, or colleague. A time of a lot of emotion, it tends to cause wrinkles around your eyes as you struggle with the difficult feelings.

I had one student who was well into her 50s but had few if any wrinkles around her eyes. I finally had to ask her what the decade of her 30s was like for her. "Oh, I spent the entire ten years living in a spiritual community, meditating nearly nonstop!" she replied. That certainly wasn't the kind of activity or environment that would stimulate a lot of difficult emotions and form lines.

Nose = 40s

This is a yang, Mountain decade, oriented more outward after the inner struggle of the 30s. It's often a time when people make a name for themselves and finally achieve success in their careers. Because of this emphasis on external achievement, it's not as much a period of focus on emotional work, and so the nose will develop few wrinkles or markings to indicate that kind of stress. Of course, troubles do happen in any decade; and in the 40s, they'll show up as changes in the flesh of the nose or lines across the bridge.

A friend's husband had a series of horizontal lines down the entire length of his nose. Throughout his 40s he encountered a number of major setbacks in life—losing his job, having to declare bankruptcy, and enduring drug rehabilitation and the loss of a child all in that one decade.

If your nose is prominent and strong in relation to the rest of the features on your face, your 40s are a very positive time. This is often when you finally achieve a level of accomplishment in your job or start a new, more balanced life after the internal processing of your 30s. It's not uncommon to have a significant break with the past at the start of this decade, with a divorce, job change, or overall shift of focus. If you've had such experiences, you'll probably see a horizontal wrinkle right at the very top of your nose in the area between the eyes (Fig. 9). This is another important time of transition in life, and if there's a big change at this age, the line will appear to mark the passage.

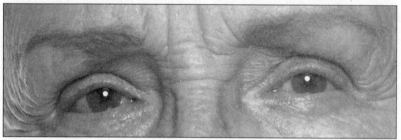

Fig. 9: The horizontal line between this woman's eyes shows a significant life change as she entered the decade of her 40s.

It's not unusual for adolescent girls to have plastic surgery to reduce the size of their noses. However, the face is still forming at that point, and the nose has actually grown faster than the rest of the features so that it looks larger than it will in a few more years! If these women had waited until their mid-20s, they would have seen the rest of the face catch up so that their noses were much more in balance with the size of their other features.

Most important, any change to the face has a corresponding energetic impact. Reducing the size of the nose can, among other things, lessen the power someone might have had in her 40s.

Mouth = 50s

It's a big drop from the end of your nose to your mouth, and the transition from the 40s to the 50s is a correspondingly dramatic one. Some advice for men as they approach their 50s is to grow a mustache to soften the landing! Women aren't fortunate enough to have that option, but by keeping their lips soft and kissable, they can achieve the same result.

My recommendation may sound like just a joke, but there's some meaning behind it. By this stage in life, built-up stress and negative emotions can cause you to hold this part of your face in a tight, tense manner. Your lips may become thin, or your entire mouth may even turn down in an unhappy curve. Keeping it soft and relaxed can help you let go of some of this tension.

The 50s is a River decade, a yin time again, and issues you've pushed down or tried to ignore in the past now come up to be looked at again, but in a different way. This time, it's likely that an imbalance might emerge physically in a way that affects your health. Some doctors call the early 50s the "Bermuda Triangle of Health," when people who never had an illness of any consequence before may face this issue.

So a major focus for this decade is taking care of yourself and finally making sure that you have what you need to feel satisfied. At this time, you can bump into the realization that your expectations haven't been met. There can be a buildup of disappointments with your partner, or life circumstances in general may have reached a point where things are too big to ignore. The most important thing to realize about this period is that it's an opportunity to examine how you may not feel nourished and figure out what to do about it. You can sink deeper into the feeling that no one has ever given you what you really wanted, or you can realize that you're fully capable of giving it to yourself.

As I stated, the most important thing to be aware of as you enter your 50s is maintaining soft lips and not holding tension there. If you keep feelings of softness and receptivity, you can't also be experiencing negativity or resentment. Instead, the message you'll be giving the outside world is one of openness and availability. This allows the possibility of emotional, spiritual, or material nourishment coming into your life. After all, how can you receive sustenance if your mouth is held tightly?

One of the easiest ways to begin to change this feature is to consciously create a slight smile several times a day. Over a short period of time, this can become natural. Studies have also shown that even faking a smile creates the same endorphins in the body that a genuine one does. So you can actually be increasing your feelings of happiness by remembering to make even a small expression of pleasure several times a day!

For women, the 50s is often a time of dealing with the additional challenges of menopause. Physical and emotional difficulties can be huge obstructions to feeling soft and receptive! Remembering that this is a time of transition and not an end point can be important; allowing yourself to flow with change rather than resist it is often a huge new lesson, with an impact extending far beyond these few years. Cultivating a soft mouth can provide a wonderful ripple effect throughout your system and help you navigate life's natural alterations more easily.

So in your 50s, your job is to go to the next level of giving yourself the life you truly want. You may not have been aware of how much work you've already done and only see the pieces that are still missing. Softening toward the world and letting go of what you've been carrying allows what you've been struggling to find to drop into your lap.

Chin = 60s

Your chin indicates what the decade of your 60s will be like. This is another Mountain period, after you've passed through the emotional and/or physical turmoil of your 50s. A strong, prominent chin in comparison to the rest of the features on your face indicates a positive decade. However, if you don't have one, that doesn't mean it will be a bad decade, just that it won't be as powerful as some in the past or some yet to come.

It's not uncommon to have markings or wrinkles develop on your chin by the time you reach your 60s. This seems to be especially true for people who also have markings on the mouth. If there are strong difficulties in the 50s, sometimes these show up again in a new or deeper form in the following decade, giving you another opportunity to work through old issues. Alternatively, if you make dramatic change while still in your 50s, you may see a diminishment of any markings on your chin. In this case, the shifts you made while in your 50s changed what was to come in the next ten years.

If you've encountered strong challenges in your life, by the time you're entering your 60s you may have used up a lot of willpower in order to deal with them. There could be resulting markings on your chin to indicate that this decade is time to take care with your energy level and health. Being mindful of the level of your "reservoir" of energy throughout life is always important, but even more so in your 60s if your chin is small compared to the rest of your features or has developed noticeable wrinkles or markings.

One thing you see frequently on people's chins is a horizontal line partway between the mouth and the bottom of the chin (Fig. 10). This indicates a break with the past, a time when there's a change in life. It's sometimes also called the "retirement line," as the mid-60s is often when people leave the professional world, a definite departure from their earlier years.

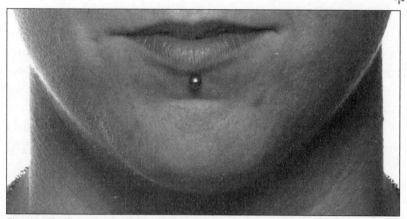

Fig. 10: The horizontal wrinkle at this point on the chin reflects a life change in the decade of the 60s.

Jaw = 70s

Both right and left sides of the jaw represent your experience in your 70s. A strong and/or well-defined jaw indicates a positive decade. Any markings there show you at what stages you'll be dealing with life issues yet again.

This time is often a very powerful phase of letting go. Sometimes this involves literally releasing possessions in order to move to be near family, to have a smaller home, or to transition from independent living to a retirement home or assisted-living facility. It can also be a mental shift as you change priorities or allow new ways of looking at relationships, which can occur when old conflicts are finally resolved or released. The 70s can be a time of beginning to turn inward, to focus on refining what you want your life to be in its final stages.

Sides of Face = 80s and 90s

The 80s is shown on the right side of a woman's face, and the 90s on the left. For men, it's reversed: the 80s on their left and 90s on their right. In this stage of life, there's less emphasis on Mountains and Rivers—rather, there's a continuation of the work begun in the 70s. These years are the next phase, which is one of further contraction into your essence. As you get older, you just become a more condensed version of yourself. Your responsibility is to let the sweetness condense, instead of any negativity.

As with the other decades, you'll look for any wrinkles, markings, or discolorations to show you where challenges or stress might be encountered. Although you usually have many wrinkles by the time you reach this age, it's not a bad thing! Every line means something: an experience acknowledged, an emotion felt, or a lesson learned, all of which are part of your passage as you travel on your life's journey.

Bottom of Chin = 99/100

The point where you complete your first 100 years is on the underside of the chin. From there on, you start all over again!

The Four Turning Points

The Chinese actually believe that the most important phases of life are the movements between the decades. And of those, face reading teaches that the really significant shifts don't begin until you enter your 40s. These transitions are called the "Four Turning Points," or "Four Gates."

The first point or gate is between your eyebrows, marking when you enter your 40s and move into the stage where you really begin to define your place in the world. The second is on your philtrum (the groove above your upper lip) as you commence your 50s, a phase where you examine what you need out of life that you haven't yet gotten. The third is under your lower lip as you transit into your 60s, when it's common to retire, slow down, or make other major changes. And the fourth is at the bottom of your chin as you enter your 70s, a time of letting go and turning inward.

So your face shows you where you've come from and where you're going, based on who you are in the present moment. There's actually a point on your face to indicate each year of your life, as illustrated on the male and female facial maps on the following pages (Figs. 11 and 12). You can use the diagrams to investigate the possible meaning of a specific marking. For instance, if you have a deep horizontal wrinkle in the center of your forehead, this could be related to your first intense romantic relationship at age 21. A spot by your eyebrow could mark giving birth to your first child when you were 32.

There might also be more than one marking to denote an experience that lasted for some time, such as a difficult marriage. In that case, your face might show the years that were the most stressful, or even have a series of traces to record the entire experience for the period it lasted. One recent client of mine had a small horizontal wrinkle on his forehead at the point indicating age 26, which was when his marriage began, a deeper wrinkle when his wife had an affair when he was 28, and a final indentation by his eye at age 39 when the union ended in a difficult divorce.

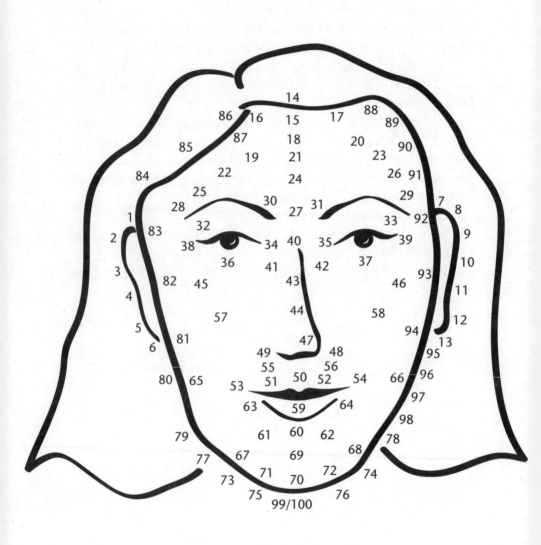

Fig. 11: Female Facial Map

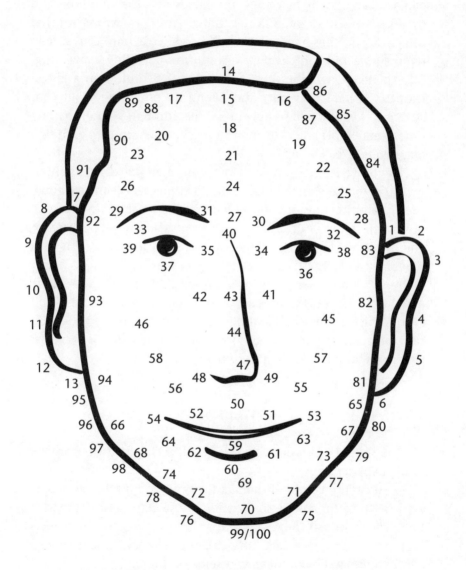

Fig. 12: Male Facial Map

Markings

As you read the odyssey of your life on your face, undoubtedly you'll see many markings: wrinkles, scars, discolorations, and the like. None of these indicates that anything is "wrong" or that something bad has happened or will happen! Each imprint simply represents a moment in your adventure, indicating a meaningful experience, whether positive or negative, and often a lesson learned. Perhaps only with the careful documenting of all your adventures would you be able to go back through your entire lifetime to remember and explain what specific event formed each sign upon your face.

As you've learned, the body and mind are inextricably intertwined. A marking on your face can sometimes reflect an emotional stress, a physical one, or both. When you're evaluating the meaning of something on your face, you'll probably know what's true for you. When you're reading someone else, you can explore this with them by asking questions.

Face reading doesn't give much weight to small and subtle markings, which most of them are. Instead, the major signs—and even more so, the actual features on your face—are more significant in revealing who you are now and your wonderful potential to express your true calling from here.

Wrinkles

You should feel proud of your wrinkles! They're the reflections of life experienced, authentic emotions felt, and wisdom gained. The goal isn't to get rid of them, although I do find that as people work on their difficult personal issues, those marks associated with them can diminish (more about that later). The goal is to understand the meaning of each line, because this new awareness will allow you to accept and love yourself a bit more.

There tend to be three kinds of people who have few wrinkles despite their age. One major group are those who live only from the neck up, totally out of touch with their feelings. Experiencing emotions is what creates most of these marks as we make expressions on our faces over and over again. If it's not safe to feel, you'll suppress your emotions and not create lines. I've had women clients with few wrinkles who had been in abusive marriages lasting many years. They'd stifled themselves so that they wouldn't have to feel the tremendous pain of such a life and thus ended up with smooth faces (and shut-down hearts).

One client endured a childhood with virtually no nurturing. His mother's mental illness had gone out of control soon after his birth, and he was sent away from the United States, bouncing among a series of relatives in Europe and being treated more like a burden than a child to love. He was never given a room or even a bed of his own. He had to adjust to various new schools, countries, and even languages. When, as a teenager, he was finally delivered back to his mother, he was allowed to sleep on a bed in her den. But every morning, he had to take the sheets and blankets off because his mother liked to look at the lovely mattress during the day! He wasn't allowed to remake the bed until he went to sleep each night. So even when he was reunited with his mother, he still didn't feel he had a soft, solid place to call his own.

His face at 58 was nearly devoid of wrinkles. He was aware he'd stifled the hurt child's feelings over a lifetime and was actively involved in personal-growth work to deal with gently getting in touch with those emotions. He excitedly contacted me a few weeks after our consultation to say that wrinkles had suddenly started appearing on his face! He took this as a sign that he was truly believing that it was safe to feel again, and he was confident that most of the wrinkles would probably diminish as he accepted these emotions and let them go.

A second reason someone has no wrinkles could be that he has lived a very sheltered existence, having few experiences that would cause strong emotions. Sometimes if someone like this has a trauma, he can wrinkle excessively in a very short period of time. If he hasn't learned how to deal with stress and has no idea how to cope with the strong emotions, he'll mark his face suddenly and dramatically.

One of my students was a 62-year-old man who was so inherently anxious that he'd kept his life very small. He still lived in the house he grew up in, selected a profession he could work at in solitude, and had never had a close relationship. His face was so unnaturally youthful, it was virtually unmarked. He came to my workshop because after such a reclusive existence, he finally felt ready to have a wider experience of life. Interestingly, his strongest feature was his chin, which is associated with the decade of the 60s and (as I'll discuss later in this book) his willpower. So, upon reaching the age indicated by his chin, he finally found the courage to begin to fulfill his need to step into life more fully.

The third type of person with few wrinkles is of another sort entirely. She has learned how not to hold on to issues. She may have lines come and go because she can accept and then release feelings as they arise. I tend to believe that the only bad emotion is a stuck emotion. If you're clinging to certain feelings and getting lost in them on a regular basis, or if you don't manage them in a balanced way, energetic "stuckness" will develop. But this person has found ways to keep anything from getting lodged in her system and blocking her energy.

If you have a wrinkle on your face that's bothering you, there's an experiment you can do in order to help you find out what it's related to. Put a piece of adhesive tape on the wrinkle and wear it for a few hours. (You may want to pick a time when you can be alone!) When you feel the tape pull, you're making the expression that's creating the line. Stop yourself, tune in, and ask yourself what you're feeling and thinking about. It's possible that you'll be able to identify a pattern of one or more specific emotions repeating each of those times. This can be an interesting exercise in dealing with an underlying issue and finding a way to move through it. As you do so, you may see the wrinkle diminish or even disappear. If stress is being held emotionally, it will also be held in the body; when it's released, the physical self will also show that change.

— **Horizontal wrinkles:** What happens to you in life tends to create horizontal wrinkles across your face. Good stress has an impact just like the bad does—remember, it's not what happens so much as how you feel about it after all. You'll mark the important times: when you got married or divorced, the death of your parents, and the birth of your children. Your face can show your difficult relationships, when you endured military training or medical school, or when your dog ran away, if that was an important experience in your life.

— **Vertical wrinkles:** Remember when your mother used to say, "Don't make that face—what if it froze that way?!" There's some truth to that. We tend to have patterns of expressions associated with certain emotions that we experience repetitively. If you make any motion repeatedly over a period of time, it will gradually carve itself into your face. Most marks caused by this are vertical. For instance, it's very common to see two upright lines between someone's eyebrows. These come from one of two combinations: frustration and anger or intense concentration and effort, usually with tension held around a thought or feeling.

Freckles and Moles

If you have just a few freckles on your face, these are usually considered the small, subtle markings that denote the timing of a life event or lesson. You can locate the age the event happened by referring to the facial map. If your face has lots of freckles, however, you fall into the specific category of the Fire Element that we'll cover in Chapters 9 and 10.

Moles are another special category, as the Chinese considered most of them to be important. We'll talk about moles in Chapters 13 and 14, which are about the Metal Element.

Scars

As opposed to an impression like a wrinkle, a scar at a certain point on your face can be an indicator of a life issue to be worked on. The body holds on to certain things for a set time and then brings them to awareness in order to give you an opportunity to work through them.

As you saw on the facial map, every age of your life is represented by an area of your face. If you have a scar, you can check to see the age associated with the place the scar is located. If it's at an age that you've already passed, then you might think back to what you were experiencing at that time in order to understand why your face marked it as an important phase in your life. Remember that this may not be exact; it may be within a year either way of the actual age represented on the facial map.

If you see a scar at an age you haven't yet reached—for instance, if you're 29 and there's a scar at the place on your face that has to do with age 50, it indicates an issue that has a "shelf life" ending at that time. In other words, 50 is its "pull date," the time when it will come up again to be examined and dealt with. It's likely that you'll experience something at that age that will be a lesson for you with respect to that issue, a new opportunity to finally move through it and release it from your life experience.

Here's how face reading looks at the meaning of any scar: Suppose when you were nine, you fell off your bike and got a scar on your cheek. At that time in your life, your parents were getting divorced and your father moved to a distant city. Perhaps the emotions that were current for you then were about feeling abandoned and unsafe.

If the mark on your cheek is at the place indicated on the facial map as age 37, for example, something might happen then to help you resolve the unprocessed emotions left over from when you were nine. It might be that your lover leaves you or your father dies, for instance. The marking shows the point in your life when you'll be given a chance—like it or not—to come to terms with those issues and do some important work on them.

So in this case, if you haven't processed that childhood experience by the age of 37, you won't have a choice—something will happen to bring those feelings to your attention. But you do have the opportunity, of course, to work on those life lessons at any stage before that time in your life. If you do so, it's very possible that when you reach 37, you won't have an experience of any great intensity surrounding that issue, and it's also possible that your scar will fade or become less noticeable. The face is always just a representation of what's going on within.

While in Paris years ago, I had dinner with an exiled princess from a Middle Eastern country. Years before, her father was assassinated in a coup, and she had to flee to France. Her entire family broke apart because of the trauma of the experience, and she was isolated and unhappy. She asked me to do a face reading for her, and she was fascinated by the information and confirmed that everything I said was true . . . until one point in our conversation. I looked at her philtrum (the groove above her upper lip), which was long and well defined. The Chinese consider this a sign of long life, so I mentioned it to her. Suddenly, it was as if a door had slammed shut in my face. She sat bolt upright in her chair and said, "Oh, no, I know that's not right. I am going to die at the age of 63."

When I asked her why she thought that, she replied, "Because my father was assassinated at the age of 63, and I know I am destined to die at that age as well." Well, there wasn't much I could say to that! So I softly commented that her face didn't indicate this and moved on. She shifted in her seat at that point, and the light revealed a scar on her chin that I hadn't seen before.

What chilled my blood at that moment was that the mark was at the place denoting age 63 in her life. "Where did you get that scar on your chin?" I asked.

"I got it in a car accident on the night my father was killed," she replied. And so there we had the physical evidence on her face that at age 63 she was scheduled to deal with whatever emotional issues she had around her father's assassination and the breakup of her family. I didn't believe it meant that she was going to die, but she certainly would have the opportunity to work through this powerful issue at that time.

A scar on one of the major features of your face also has the effect of diminishing the power that feature symbolizes. For instance, a scar on your eyebrow can affect your level of confidence, for as I'll discuss later, this is one aspect of your personality that body part represents.

Individual markings can be fascinating indicators of what life has brought you and what's still to come. But far more important are two things: lines made from repeated expressions and the actual features on your face. And in order to understand those, we now need to move more deeply into the ancient foundation upon which face reading is based.

Part II

THE
WISDOM

"To a true
artist only that face
is beautiful which, quite
apart from its exterior,
shines with the truth
within the soul."

— MAHATMA GANDHI

Chapter 4

UNIVERSAL PRINCIPLES

You now enter the most important part of your journey. Here you'll learn the principles on which this wisdom is based and then travel deeper through each of the five Elemental or archetypal qualities that shine through your face. There are two sample portraits for each of the five different Elements, followed by two chapters for each one. In the first, you'll explore a general overview of that personality and learn a broad range of the ways it can be expressed in your life. In the second, you'll discover techniques to recognize how that energy presents itself in your face.

One note about the photographs, from the full-face portraits to those focusing on the smaller details: Each image is only meant to illustrate an example of how a face, feature, or marking could be displayed. You don't need to have *exactly* the same detail on your face in order to possess the quality described. Use these images as guides, not dictators.

Chinese philosophy holds a secret knowledge so powerful that it could change your life. This ancient wisdom evolved over thousands of years of scientific observation of the cycles of man

and nature, the equivalent of the greatest period of "research and development" ever known.

What the Chinese discovered were the universal principles that underlie all of life—the simple, elegant understanding of how people, places, and the world as a whole function. Over the centuries, this wisdom came to be concealed within mythology and superstition or buried in dry medical texts. But it lay like hidden treasure as the heart of the Chinese understanding of how the universe works. Face reading is based on this same ancient Taoist foundation that forms the basis of acupuncture and Chinese medicine. It's a part of this simple, elegant, and accessible understanding of all creation.

So now I'd like to share with you, not entirely tongue in cheek, the Meaning of Life:

Over thousands of years, the ancient Chinese observed nature. They watched the cycle of time repeat over and over each day: night, morning, noon, afternoon, and evening. They saw the seasons change: the cold stillness of winter, the vitality of spring, the full bloom of summer, early autumn with ripe fruit falling from the trees, and late autumn when the leaves fall and plants seem to wither and die. They noticed how humankind moves through life: the baby floating in utero; the little child full of energy; the prime of life when the body is at its physical peak; then middle age, when everyone begins to slow down; and old age, as we fade toward death.

What the Chinese came to see is that all life moves in a circle, a beautifully defined passage from beginning through to the end and then beginning all over again. And as they observed this natural circular flow, repeating over and over, they began to discern different phases that everything moves through in traversing this path. The energy of dawn is nothing like that of late afternoon, and the lushness of summer isn't the same as the depth of winter. The energy of a child is very different from what it will be when he's old and frail.

So as life or energy moves in this circle, it has different qualities at different stages; it changes as it moves. The Chinese defined five different stages of change and gave them descriptive names: Water, Wood, Fire, Earth, and Metal. This doesn't mean that the ancient Chinese thought the universe was physically made up of these substances; the names were merely symbolic of the type of energy at various places in the cycle. These symbols, or archetypes, came to be called the Five Elements or the Five Phases.

Like the seasons, times of day, and times of life, we're personally subject to the same cycle and laws of nature. The movement of the Five Elements holds true for everything in existence—our life spans, a meal, a business meeting, a breath, our bodies, our personalities—all of creation can be understood within this beautiful, elegant pattern. Understanding this cycle is important because it shows us the structure of change and regularity that's the true constant of life. It's a coherent harmony that we can work with to integrate ourselves with the natural rhythms of the universe.

This understanding of the Five Elements dates back to the 2nd or 3rd millennium B.C.E. (The oldest remaining records come from the 3rd and 4th centuries B.C.E.) It's an ancient and sophisticated system of perceiving how life works that carries enormous depth, and the study of the Five Elements is a lifelong adventure. But like

all well-developed knowledge, it's also easy to immediately begin to apply in practical ways, so let's take a moment to get a clear sense of each Element.

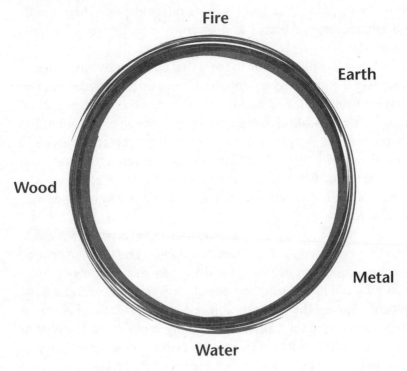

Fig. 14: The Five-Element Cycle

— **Water = night, winter, death, and prebirth.** This Element is the energy of the hibernation and dormancy of winter, as well as the stillness of night. It's the vibration of death, but also of prebirth—of the baby floating in the amniotic fluid, the seed germinating underground. Water is a dark, still, quiet energy, yet with powerful potential.

— **Wood = morning, spring, birth, and childhood.** This Element is the drive to be alive, the force of spring and the plants bursting through the ground. It's morning at dawn when all life is stirring—birth and growth; the dynamic energy all children have as they run and shout. Wood is strong, upward-moving energy.

— **Fire = noon, summer, and the prime of life.** This Element is the summer when all the plants are at their peak—noon, when the sun is directly above and the heat is most intense. Fire is when we're fully grown and are at our greatest physical power. It's peaking energy, moving upward and outward in expansion.

— **Earth = afternoon, late summer/early fall, and middle age.** This Element is harvest time, when the fruit is ripe and dropping off the trees. It's afternoon, a slower time as the day begins to settle. This is when we reach middle age, start to slow down, and can begin to reap the rewards of our hard work. The energy of Earth is downward moving, consolidating, heavier.

— **Metal = early evening, late fall, and old age.** This Element is the fall after the harvest, when the leaves are dropping and bare twigs are etched across the gray sky. It's that time of day when we finish the last of our work so we can rest in the evening. This is the point in life when we begin to fade and feel it necessary to conserve our strength, and refine the last details of our time here. Metal is inward-moving energy, contracting, condensing, and hardening.

So everything begins with Water, and each Element nurtures the one coming after. Just as spring arises from winter or the baby is born from the womb, Water energy becomes Wood energy. An easy way to remember how the cycle goes is this: Water feeds plants, so Wood can grow. Wood feeds Fire, which burns to ash, creating Earth. The Earth forms ore and gems, hard rocks, creating Metal. Metal's minerals give Water its richness, the rocks provide a riverbed for Water to flow, and the cycle continues.

It seems simple, this explanation of the pattern of all life; and in fact, it's a universal principle that's easy to understand and use. If you continue to study and play with it, you'll see that the Five Elements can be applied to anything—the timeline of a relationship, the layout of your home, the experience of an emotion, how organizations change over time, and even your phases of reading this book. But the simplicity is also deceptive! You can explore the

Five Elements for the rest of your life and still find new levels of understanding. This, to me, is the sign of its power and validity.

But how can this cycle have anything to do with personality? And how could that be discerned on someone's face? We all have some of each of the Five Elements, but usually one or two of them are emphasized in our nature, and these will be able to be seen on the face.

The Five Elements, as explored in face reading, can give you the answer to those two important questions posed at the beginning of this book: *Who are you? What is your calling?* They'll show you where your emotional strengths are, as well as your inherent tendencies to respond to life in certain ways. They'll also reveal where you're challenged and why you may notice patterns of experience repeating over and over in your life. But with that comes a realization of how to transform what you experience as a negative into an understood and loved aspect that can be integrated in a balanced way into the wholeness of who you are.

Reading the Elements presented on your face can also give you insight into your physical health, with clues to the underlying emotional basis for any physical imbalance. This book isn't intended to be used for diagnosis in any way, but it may give you information about any health challenges you may have had in the past or be experiencing currently.

So let's start at the beginning of the cycle with Water.

Chapter 5

WATER—TO BE

In this chapter, I'll introduce the basics of the Water Element, and you'll learn how to identify it. To begin, here's a quick-reference list of Water characteristics:

- **Energy:** dark, still, floating, quiet, night, winter, death, prebirth

- **Qualities:** wise, courageous, fearful, tenacious, determined, willful, independent, strong, melancholic, stubborn, mysterious, reflective, dreamy, artistic, secretive, single-minded, dramatic, unorthodox, philosophical, intuitive, slow to process issues, needs freedom

- **Major features:** ears, hairline, upper forehead, under-eye area, philtrum, chin

- **Organs:** kidney, bladder

- **Sense organ:** ears

What to Look for

You don't need to have *all* of the following aspects for this Element to play a strong role in your life—any of these will indicate that it's a factor in your personality. The more of them you possess, the more Water there is in your nature:

- Broad or high, domed forehead
- Distinct shadowing above and/or below the eyes; dreamy, mysterious-looking eyes
- Well-defined philtrum
- Strong, prominent chin
- Large ears and/or earlobes
- Large hips and/or slight plumpness or softness to the face and body, with no sharp features
- Large, strong bones (thick wrists and ankles), healthy teeth
- Thick or wavy lustrous hair
- Black undertone to complexion

Fig. 15: Water Face

Fig. 16: Water Face

How do you know if the Water Element is a major part of your personality? You look for your strongest features—what's most noticeable in your face. You may not have all or even many of the kinds of features listed above, but if one of the first things you notice is your strong chin or shadowing around your eyes, you have this Element in your makeup. The more strong Water features you have, the more of this energy you have in your personality.

If you're a typical Water person, you might have a high, rounded forehead and a prominent chin. You may also be slightly plump overall, almost as if your body is retaining water; and thick, strong wrists and ankles. Your hips could be wide, your eyes shadowed, your hair thick and lustrous, and your ears or earlobes large. If you have all of these characteristics, which is rare, you will know that you're a very Watery individual!

Well-known faces that show the Water Element include: Jay Leno, George Clooney, Reese Witherspoon, Christina Ricci, Elvis Presley, and Jon Stewart.

Water Energy and Power

The energy of Water is deep and powerful. It's the seed germinating underground in the cold depths of winter and the baby floating silently in amniotic fluid . . . it's the mystery of life. It's also the mystery of death and the dark abyss, the great unknown to which everything ultimately returns.

The power of this Element is hidden. You can't perceive the seed beneath the earth, let alone its immense potential, nor can you see the unborn infant or the power of drama it can tolerate in the birth experience. You can't witness infinity waiting past death.

Water is the floating dreaminess of the pre- and postlife state of being. It isn't in the physical world as such—it has to do with night and the dreams that arise from the depths of the subconscious. The energy of this Element is dark, deep, mysterious, and powerful. It can be the infinite peace of a reflective pool, the intense torrent of a flood, the endurance of the perpetual tides, or the eternal patience of a single drip carving out a canyon. All of these have a deep impact in their own way.

This part of the cycle isn't about doing, but rather is a state of *being,* and therefore the verb that best describes the quality of Water is *to be.* A Water Element person carries that deep sense of infinity, that hidden power of being within his or her personality.

The Personality of Water

For each Element, there are personal qualities that are assets and ones that are challenges. Some of Water's most important strengths are incredible inner courage, tenacity, determination, and willpower that surpass any other Element's.

There's also an innate wisdom, the ability to touch at a very deep level what the primal mystery of life is truly about. If you are a Water person, you have a depth of feeling that others rarely access. This, along with your inner courage, can be your source of success in life. Through Water's natural courage and wisdom, you can summon the strength and determination to move forward and explore life in an adventurous way. You also have the power to handle the intensity of another person's strongest feelings and hold the space for their doing deep personal work.

The challenge for this Element is the emotion of fear, which will show up during stressful times. Remember that Water is about the void, the vast beginning and ending place where there are no boundaries and all is dark and undefined. It would be natural, then, for dread to arise in the face of such a limitless, unknown land.

Fear can make your Water freeze in place, and you'll find yourself unable to move forward. You may also feel as though you're swirling around in a little whirlpool, unable to make a decision or take action. Water often responds to fear by withdrawing and becoming cautious or even secretive, unable to speak up to resolve a problem. In my work with Water people, I often see that one very common challenge for them is finding their voice, being able to declare their truth, or speaking up for themselves despite their feelings. If this sounds familiar, the key to this situation is to access your incredible Elemental courage and determination that can give you the strength to feel the fear but not be paralyzed by it.

Because of this tendency toward secretiveness, silence, or withdrawing when upset, it may be the case that if someone has hurt your feelings, he may never know it. You'll tend not to talk about it or share it with him; and in the end, the relationship can falter because of the hidden hurts you're not able to acknowledge.

I've had Water people quote to me verbatim what someone said 20 years before that had pierced their hearts. Yet they'd never told those who hurt them, and possibly the relationship had ended at that point because they weren't able to speak up to resolve their feelings.

This isn't about holding a grudge—that has to do with anger. Nor is it not about being overly emotional. As a Water person, you truly feel things more deeply and are affected by those emotions

64

more than other people. There's a lot going on under the surface with your Element, an incredible depth of feeling that's both your greatest strength and biggest challenge. It's what gives you the richness of your experience in life, yet also provides the intensity that at times can be almost too much to bear.

The easiest way to spot this is your Watery tendency to cry at the drop of a hat! If you find that little things make your eyes well up or if tears come in the middle of an everyday conversation, a TV commercial, or in a moment of emotion, you can be sure that you have some of this Element in your personality. Again, it's not a sign of weakness at all, but rather an indication of how deeply you experience life. As Water, you'll process experiences through crying, living life with tears at the ready.

I was glad to have this information when I had a very Watery assistant. She'd arrive at work many days with tears streaming down her face, but I knew that this didn't mean I should send her home for a mental-health day. Rather, she'd just had a moving phone conversation on the way to work or remembered something she'd experienced the day before that had touched her deeply.

But in most professions, this quality can make life difficult. Tears in a staff meeting or while talking with a client can result in other people assuming you're overly emotional or unable to handle the pressure. This can be a terrible challenge, especially for men in our culture. If only the corporate world recognized the value of having employees who aren't just alive from the neck up! As it is right now, Water people's complementary ability to keep their feelings hidden is what helps them survive in most of the business world.

If you're part of this Element, you're probably fascinated with that sense of mystery to life and uncovering the truth deep within it. Water is the fertile space without boundaries where anything can happen and creativity can thrive. You're the dreamy, creative person—the artist, writer, musician, or philosopher. Or you may be the intuitive, who plumbs the depth of the sea of consciousness to bring answers to the surface. This element is that nonlinear place of no time or space, where knowledge can be accessed immediately and intuition that gives you the "knowing before you know" information.

You can also be the successful businessperson who always has a creative way to flow around any obstacle put in your path or the parent who easily adjusts to your baby's needs. Water doesn't flow in straight lines, and you'll know how to wiggle with the stream of life or you'll use your tenacity to surge on through.

In fact, the one thing you should know about Water is that freedom is of utmost importance. Confinement is like death! Restrictions of any kind don't fit well with the need to flow. If you're very Watery, you do *not* want to take a job where you have to clock in by 9:00 A.M. and can't leave until 5:01 P.M. You may end up working in unusual positions that give you flexible hours, or you could start a business so that you can set your own schedule and do what you want, when you want.

In fact, you'll tend to have an unusual life overall. Your career may be out of the norm, or you may travel frequently—whether you like it or not! You may find that you end up living in many places in your life or in an exotic part of the world. Water flows, explores, and doesn't stand still; and the tendency is always to move toward the mystery and away from the mundane.

This Element's favorite position is horizontal. You love to lie down, whether lounging in bed reading a book, lying on the couch, tapping on your laptop, or soaking in the bathtub. In my feng-shui work with any Water client, I don't have to ask where she spends most of her working time, even if she has a home office. She may own a desk, but you can bet that her most productive time is spent in bed or on the couch. I often suggest buying a recliner or couch for her office, as it gives her a space that reflects her needs and—at the very least—an opportunity to refresh her Water throughout the day.

This is an important piece of knowledge: Each Element has its own energetic need—a movement or a feeling that should be frequently nurtured and allowed to exist every day. If you're Water, the point isn't to make yourself be less Watery. Rather, you must create a way to frequently bring in that surge of specific energy that feeds your soul. You need to express, nourish, and enhance your Element. I don't make a Water woman sit upright on a hard chair at a tiny desk to work—I allow her the most Watery work space possible.

But because of this need for more of a flowy kind of lifestyle, you can drive others in your life up the wall! You'll probably have a tendency to be late, for there are no clocks on the Water planet, and a linear concept of time can be foreign to you. You don't have a tight focus, but instead an inherent dreaminess, an inner flow that has nothing to do with keeping track of the passing minutes. Therefore, it's very difficult for you to get used to this dissonant requirement to be in a certain place at an exact time.

In fact, one of my students told me that I virtually saved her marriage with this information. She'd shown me a photograph of her husband, who was one of the most Watery men I'd ever seen. She said that I described his personality exactly, but what stirred her most was the explanation of his lateness. She said it had been driving her crazy—he never showed up anywhere when he was supposed to, no matter how hard he tried. She knew his behavior wasn't purposeful, but she couldn't understand how a highly intelligent man could possibly not be aware of the time passing. (Now of course, there *are* people with passive-aggressive tendencies who are late for unconsciously hostile reasons; not everyone who's chronically tardy falls into this Element!)

After understanding how his Water personality might factor into the equation, she was able to stop taking his actions so personally and see him in a different light. Rather than get upset if he didn't arrive on time to meet her, she said, "I just learned to bring a book!" Although it sounds simplistic, what was important was that she'd released her judgment and hurt and stopped standing there fuming every time she had to wait for him. Instead, she arranged to meet where she knew there would be a comfy chair so that she could enjoy her book, knowing he'd arrive eventually. Much of the tension in their relationship evaporated just due to this one revelation.

Other ways that this tendency to "flow" can drive others crazy is in conversation. As Water, you won't speak quickly, nor do you always come to the point very efficiently. Instead, you'll tend to wander as you speak and sometimes talk all around a subject. It can drive non-Water people up the wall, waiting for you to cut to the chase. Even a shopping trip may have you walking slowly in

curving paths throughout a store, pausing here and there and probably exasperating some of your companions. Water doesn't move in straight lines.

This circuitous process can show up in more important areas, too. If you're Water, you'll feel best if you can make a decision slowly or work on a problem quietly over time. You'll need to let things take their natural course, allow all of the aspects of an issue to seep down through every layer of your consciousness, and let the answer form gradually, like a baby gestating in the womb. It will be stressful if you're forced to make a sudden decision or come to a quick conclusion, as it will feel completely against your nature. At the very least, you'll rely on your intuition for answers as much as your logical brain.

In daily life, you'll love to stay up late into the dark stillness of the night and to sleep late, immersed in your dreams. You may find it difficult to emerge in the morning, preferring to wake up slowly and not suddenly break the connections with the ethereal world you've been floating in all night. In fact, you may feel as though you don't quite leave your dreams behind, even when you're up and out of bed; strands will cling to you like cobwebs long after you're awake.

Privacy is also very important to this Element, and even if you're extroverted, you'll need time alone to be quiet. Meditation often comes more easily for you than many others, as you find it easy to sink into that still place inside.

Water Style

— **Clothing:** We've all watched the beautiful sensual flow of a river, taken a long drink of cool water and felt it move down inside us, or sunk into a deep bathtub with a luxurious sigh. You can see this sensuality in the clothes that Water wears. If you're a Water woman, you may love flowy clothes and cover yourself from neck to ankle in some softly beautiful outfit, probably with a trailing scarf or velvet jacket. Your thick, lustrous hair may be worn long and wavy. Ethnic or artistic fashions are your preference, and blues and blacks are common Water colors. And because of your need for freedom and your creative tastes, you'll probably choose footwear that you can kick off easily or else one-of-a-kind, handmade shoes that cost $500—but completely feed your soul.

— **Home:** For your environment, your Water Element likes . . . water! You'll tend to prefer to live near a lake, river, or ocean, and it's even better if you can see it directly from your home. You'll prefer open-plan abodes that allow your line of sight to flow from space to space, rather than small, cozy rooms. You may have artwork with images of water or abstracts with fluid lines. Your décor is sensual and unusual, with velvet curtains or plush upholstery and ornaments from exotic places or indigenous cultures.

Your favorite place in the house could be the bedroom because of your love of being horizontal—I've seen Water people virtually swoon when they describe their top-quality mattresses. Or if not the bedroom, then certainly the bathroom is the favorite place, as this Element often considers it essential to end each day with a long soak in the tub.

Because Water also has to do with darkness, you'll thrive in environments where there can be some dark corners, some mystery in places. My mother is an extremely Watery artist whose home shows all the beautiful aspects of her creativity. There's very little bright overhead lighting, only a few table lamps here and there. This creates pools of darkness that suit her perfectly. However, I have very little Water Element, and when I'm in her home, I soon become uncomfortable in the dimness. I can't help but turn on more lights so I can feel better. I often do this automatically, but then I have to laugh when I see my mother reflexively following after me, switching everything off! We're each seeking our own balance in the environment.

— **Movement:** Even physical exercise can be personalized for each Element's best use. The forms of yoga that involve slow, flowing motions and breath are perfect for Water people. Swimming, of course, is another good activity, along with ice skating, tai chi, dancing, and anything that doesn't involve tension or forced movements.

Those in this Element don't go for "power walks," but prefer strolls or taking the dog out and rambling in meandering curves.

— **Profession:** If you're Water, you could be naturally drawn to work in creative fields such as art, music, or writing. Or you could be a brilliant therapist, with your wise and courageous ability to travel to those deep inner places and not back down from intense emotions. You also might find yourself in jobs dealing with money, such as financial planning, or in the medical profession. Dentists often have a lot of Water, as teeth are a part of the body that has to do with this Element.

You could also end up in a career that has something to do with actual water or some aspect of it. I was giving a lecture once and was questioned at the end by a man who, even though he had Watery features, said his job had nothing to do with his Element. I asked what he did for a living, and he replied that he was an attorney. This is not, in fact, a Water profession, so I was a bit stumped. Finally, I inquired about his area of practice, and he replied, "Marine law"—and he later admitted that he lived in a beach cottage and used his kayak to get to work each day!

Perhaps you've recognized yourself or a friend in the descriptions above, and it may have given you new insights and awareness. But you may feel that while you see *some* Water, it doesn't completely describe you or your friend. Remember that while we all have some of each of the five Elements in our personalities, usually one or two are emphasized—some people even have four of the Elements strongly in their faces and are weak in only one. So it may be that as you read further, you can identify a second, third, or even fourth category that gives you a complete understanding of who you are inside.

But even if you don't find Water features emphasized in your face, you still have ears, a forehead, a chin, and so on! In the next chapter, we'll examine each of these features individually and learn what they can tell us in more detail about how Water manifests in your inherent spirit.

Chapter 6

READING THE
WATER FEATURES

As I've mentioned, in addition to giving the entire face a certain look, each Element corresponds with specific facial features. In this chapter, you'll learn how to gain even more insight into the Water Element from each of these body parts.

Ears

Your ears, as you've already learned, reveal a wealth of information about what your childhood was like. But they can tell you much more.

When you came into this life, you brought with you not only your own nature, but also the inherited essence of your ancestors. Water has to do with those ancestral treasures that have been passed down to you, the reservoir of inner strength that you can draw on when your own begins to fail. The potency of this inheritance differs from person to person, and it can be read in the ears.

These body parts show the quantity of the supply of what the Chinese call the "jing" or constitution you were born with, indicating how deep that well is that you can draw on in times of need. If you have firm, large ears, this means you were born with a strong supply of rejuvenating Water, allowing you to turn to it for extra stamina and endurance.

It's been said that in recent times, ears have gotten smaller overall, and earlobes are shorter. The concern is that since the size of the feature shows the strength of your constitution, each generation has become inherently weaker. This could mean fragile immune systems, possibly compromised by environmental pollution and/ or a poorer diet, resulting in less resistance to stress and disease.

What I find interesting is that you can certainly see evidence of this recent decreasing trend. Watch any old movie from the 1940s or '50s, and you may gasp at the size of some people's ears! It's rare to see such large ones these days on anyone under the age of 60.

You can also evaluate the current state of your constitution by feeling the cartilage of your upper ears. They should be flexible but firm, the sign of a strong constitution, powerful Water *qi* (energy or life force). If they're too stiff or rigid, however, this could mean some stagnation in this Element, possibly translating as being too single-minded or intolerant or having the potential for high blood pressure.

If your ears are too thin and flexible, it can be a sign of diminished physical strength. If they're almost translucent or can be folded up quite compactly with little resistance, this can also be a sign of a delicate immune system. If yours are in this condition, you should be mindful of consistently getting true rest and renewal in your life.

The shape and size of your ears is also meaningful. The bigger they are, the stronger the supply of qi. This means you have more energy that you can take the chance of losing. So if you have large ears, you'll be able to be more of a risk taker. This played out when I watched a panel of prominent entrepreneurs being interviewed on a local television show. In one long line sat some of the more successful businesspeople in the community, and I gasped in astonishment as I realized that they all had enormous ears!

Aside from their overall size, the width of your ears also indicates how comfortable you are with taking risks. The wider they are (Fig. 17), the easier it will be for you to choose to take chances.

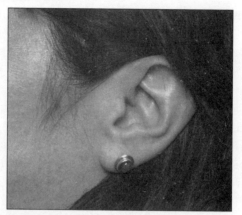

Fig. 17: Wide ears indicate someone who's comfortable taking risks.

If you have narrow ears (Fig. 18), you'll be more inclined to work in jobs that guarantee a steady income or have some stability to them. You'll also be less likely to have an interest in participating in extreme sports such as snowboarding or skydiving!

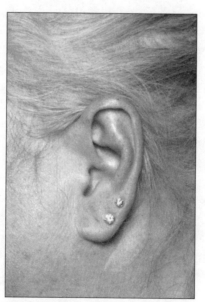

Fig. 18: Narrow ears show a need for more safety and stability.

If you have small ears, you'll tend to be more cautious and careful overall. The Chinese say that children with small ears are well behaved, which may be a reflection of the impact of fear, the emotion associated with Water. The more anxiety you feel, the more prudent you'll be.

I once had a student who had exceptionally small ears. She was a financial advisor with a reputation for being conservative and careful with her clients' money. She attracted a certain kind of customer who didn't want to be too aggressive with his investments. This was a case where a natural balance was achieved, as this woman lived in accordance with her true nature! One day, however, she shared with me some further information about her childhood, which, as you know, affects this feature.

"I grew up in a tiny one-bedroom apartment with four dysfunctional adults," she told me. "I had to stay small and quiet to avoid one of them going out of control. I believe my little ears show how much fear I lived in and how tiny I had to keep my energy." Indeed, as a child, she'd invented imaginary angels to be her friends and keep her safe because her surroundings felt so treacherous.

Where your ears are placed on your head also provides information. If the tops of your ears are at the same level as your eyebrows or above, this is said to indicate "early fame." If the tops of your ears are below your eyebrows, it will come later. In this case, "fame" can mean when you find success or your real path in life. So the higher your ears are, the more likely you are to discover this at a relatively early age. If they're low, you may be a late bloomer; it might take you a while to find your place in the world.

Earlobes

Even your earlobes can tell you about yourself. Those that look connected to the side of the head (Fig. 19) indicate that you probably maintain a connection to your family, which can be positive or negative! It may mean that you go home for a lovely Sunday dinner each week or that unhappy experiences from the past aren't yet resolved. It can also signify that even if your parents are gone, family is important to you and you need to create a sense of it wherever you go.

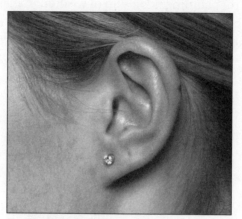

Fig. 19: Earlobes that are connected to the side of the head show a connection to family.

If you have earlobes that can be pulled away from the side of your head (Fig. 20), you can probably successfully disconnect from your relatives. Your life may be more independent, or you don't necessarily maintain close ties with family members. This shape indicates that you can create your own nurturing network with friends, rather than maintaining close biological bonds; or you may not feel a strong need for these connections in your life at all.

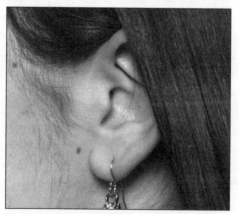

Fig. 20: Earlobes that pull away from the side of the head show the ability to separate from family.

Your earlobes are also the first of three "reservoirs of wealth" on your face. Long earlobes (Fig. 21) indicate that you naturally think about long-term planning. It's a sign of wisdom in many ways—not just having to do with finances. But if you prepare wisely for the future, it's likely that will include fiscal security as well.

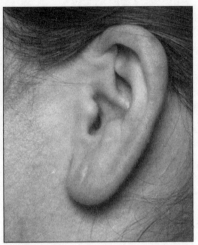

Fig. 21: Long earlobes show wisdom and long-term planning.

Small earlobes indicate that you think less about the future and live more in the present. You don't tend to look too far ahead, and it can feel a bit unnatural for you to try to. This doesn't mean that you're doomed to live in poverty in your old age! It may well be that what you're focusing on in the present is what will provide security in your later years. And because your ears continue to grow throughout your life, you always have the potential to get larger earlobes. It's also essential to remember that you can't just focus on one individual body part—all the features affect each other and can modify or control what the others are saying. It's important to always keep this in mind as you practice reading faces—yours or anyone else's.

One last thing to notice about your ears is whether they're set close to the head or stick out. Ears that lie near the side of your head indicate that you're a good listener. However, if they stick out from the sides of your head (Fig. 22), it's a mark that you don't necessarily like to do what others tell you to. People with ears that noticeably stick out tend to be highly independent.

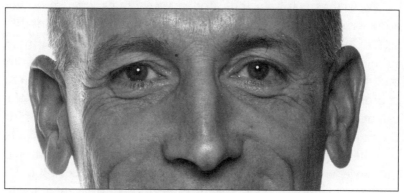

Fig. 22: Ears that stick out are the sign of an independent personality.

If your ears stick out *and* tilt forward, it's considered to be a sign that you love the sound of your own voice—in other words, you don't like to listen to others and can be quite stubborn about it. Former presidential candidate Ross Perot has these kind of ears, along with a reputation for seeming to love expressing his opinions!

I learned a deeper meaning for this feature from a client who was the author of several successful books. I noticed he had these ears and told him what this was supposed to mean. I was afraid that he'd be offended, but instead he became thoughtful. After a few moments, he said that as a writer, this made sense to him. It was actually particularly important for him to listen to his own words before sending them out into the world. He made a point of taking great care to pay attention to how a reader would perceive what he said as he wrote each draft, to be sure that he was being clear and communicating well.

With this new understanding, I watched for more of these kinds of ears and was fascinated to see that many people who are successful in the field of communications have ears that stick out and forward!

Hairline

As well as being an indicator of your life experience during adolescence (as described in Chapter 3), your hairline is another sign of Water. This part of the face is sometimes called "Mother's Influence," although it may not be specifically related to your biological mother. Rather, it has to do with whoever taught you to conform to society's rules. This kind of training often involves the use of fear, that Watery emotion, to impress on the young spirit the importance of behaving correctly.

The shape of your hairline gives an indication of this maternal influence, which is an important part of your life process. If there was a great emphasis on fear or the imposition of strict rules, it will show in a specific shape that can be easiest to see in profile (viewing yourself from the side): The sides of the hairline will come down closer to your eyebrows than is common (Fig. 23). You'll most likely have excellent manners and a high awareness of others, but it may take you longer in life to strike out for yourself or be comfortable breaking the rules.

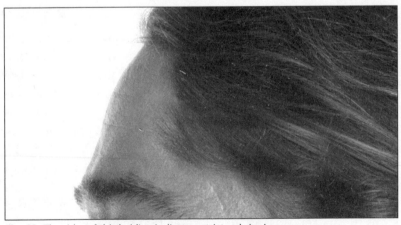

Fig. 23: The sides of this hairline indicate a strict upbringing.

Another common shape is a squared hairline, which indicates a rebellious nature (Fig. 24). If you have this one, you know that you're someone who tends to not want to obey the rules! This can be something that has created challenges for you in life, but it's also a wonderful trait because it can mean that you come up with new ideas about how to make things happen.

I often see both of these characteristics combined in the same face—a squared hairline that juts in near the eyebrows as shown in Fig. 23. It's really not surprising to see these two aspects together. It could be a result of a rebellious child's parents trying to enforce strict rules to keep him or her in line, or perhaps too much suppression created a rule breaker!

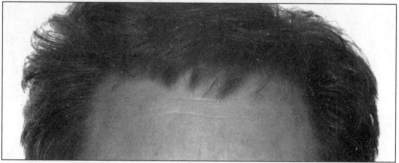

Fig. 24: A squared hairline reveals a rebellious nature.

There's a particular kind of hairline that goes back in the corners of the forehead (Fig. 25). Sometimes called the "Expansive Mind," this shows that you're open-minded overall. It also means you're not limited by rules or linear thinking, and you can extrapolate easily. Instead of having to figure something out step-by-step, you can make intuitive leaps, combining analysis and gut instinct to come to a solution. You may be the kind of person who has the answer before someone finishes asking a question or knows the punch line before he finishes telling the joke! Many scientists and philosophers have this type of hairline.

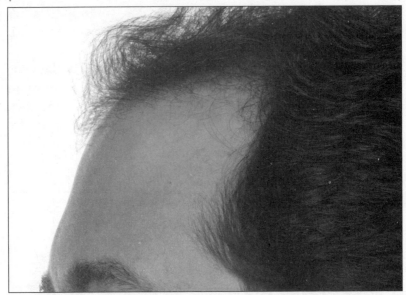

Fig. 25: This hairline represents an open mind that can make intuitive leaps.

A widow's peak or the small "V" of hairline coming down into the middle of the forehead (Fig. 26) represents enhanced charisma, creativity, and sex appeal in both men and women. This is a sign of the seductive pull of deep Water sensuality!

Fig. 26: A widow's peak hairline is a sign of extra charisma and creativity.

A receding hairline, balding from the forehead back, indicates that you have extra drive and ambition—a sign of the high testosterone level that created the hair loss. This can translate into financial success, which is why the Chinese consider it such a lucky sign.

Any unusual change to the hairline can be an indication that there's either an emotional or physical imbalance in Water. It usually shows up in a thinning of your hair along the edge of the forehead. This can simply mean that your system has been too stressed, whether by emotions, a difficult and demanding experience, or illness. It shows that your reserves are running low and you may need to recharge, often with more rest, better diet, and less stress.

Forehead

A domed and/or broad forehead is a strong sign of Water creativity. If yours curves out, you're highly creative in some way (Fig. 27). This is usually easiest to see in profile. Such a shape doesn't mean you have to be an artist—you could be an accountant—but it's a sure bet that you use your creativity in your work in some way, or that you express it through a hobby. If not, you'll probably feel unsatisfied with life until you can find some way to let those juices flow.

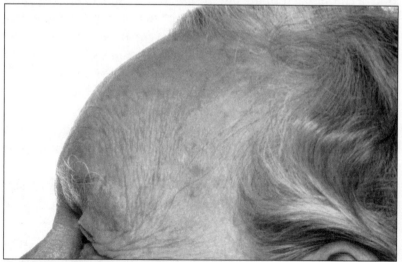

Fig. 27: A rounded forehead is a sign of a highly creative person.

The upper half of the forehead has to do with inheritance. It shows talents, skills, and abilities that have been passed down to you from your parents, grandparents, and even ancient forebears. If this part of your face is rounded or protrudes, it means that you're carrying information you've inherited from your family. The rounder the forehead, the more ancestral talents you've received. It can also indicate that you're carrying forward family "karma," some pattern of experience or a lesson that's being passed down through your lineage. This doesn't necessarily mean that you'll have the same kinds of experiences as those who came before you, but rather that there may be subtly similar life work to be done.

Occasionally you'll see something slightly different on the upper forehead that's almost like a large bump or protrusion, and it's usually more pronounced on one side than the other. In these cases, more information came predominantly from one branch of the family. The right side is associated with Mother and her ancestors, while the left has to do with Father and his relatives.

So if there's a protrusion on the left part of your forehead, it means that you've inherited traits from your father's side. At first, that may not seem like good news if you remember your dad as having terrible anger problems and you don't want to have that kind of emotional turmoil! But the important thing to keep in mind is that you've received the energy, not necessarily the same way of expressing it. Your father may not have managed his incredible drive and dynamic personality very well, expressing it through anger. You, however, may be pouring that same vitality into your career, fund-raising for charity, or any number of positive choices. No trait is good or bad; it's all in how you use it.

If there are protrusions on both the left and right sides but not the center, then you've inherited traits and talents from both your mother and father, but they're very different from each other. If your forehead is extremely rounded in the center, it means you have similar traits from both parents that could be even more enhanced in you.

It's important to pay attention to what you've received from your ancestors and not to ignore it. In fact, these talents will come up even if you resist them or think that you can't make money with them. They'll still come knocking at your door, insisting that you incorporate them into your life. The urge that comes through family traits is the natural manifestation of your ancestral qi, which is a positive thing, and you should allow it to come through. Your task may be to evolve it to a new level.

Both my parents were teachers, and it was expected that I would become one as well. As I was growing up in the 1950s and '60s, career choices for women were extremely limited: The accepted standard seemed to be that a girl could grow up to be a teacher, nurse, or secretary—only, of course, until she got married, and then she could move into her true calling as a wife and mother!

I had no desire for any of these paths and was determined to do something more interesting with my life. Many years later when my son reached the age of 13, he was grappling with thoughts of his future. Under the impression from his teachers that he had to decide on a career by the end of high school, he agonized over what to do. None of my attempts at reassuring him that he had loads of time to explore life and possibly have several different careers seemed to ease his mind.

Finally, trying to encourage him, I told him my story and how my own choices had been so limited compared to what he faced. "Grandma and Grandpa were teachers, and they thought I'd become one as well," I said. "But look at me now!" In my mind, I was viewing my journey as a writer, photographer, entrepreneur, real-estate appraiser, feng-shui practitioner, and face reader, now traveling all over the world, leading seminars and training people. . . .

"Yeah," he said, with a slightly disgusted look on his face, "you're a teacher."

My stunned expression made him smile, and I realized that he was right! All of that long, winding road had led me right back to my inheritance: teaching. So don't turn your back on the skills that come to you naturally—in the end, you'll make good use of them.

If your forehead is flatter, this doesn't mean that your ancestry has ignored you! Instead, it signifies that you can blaze a new trail and make your own way in life, perhaps even in something radically different from the rest of your family. You may be drawn to train in a new skill unlike anything your ancestors have done before you. For many people, it can be a huge relief to know that they're able to move on independently of their lineage.

A forehead that actually slants back from the brow bone is sometimes called a "dealmaker's forehead" (Fig. 28). This is someone who can think of creative solutions to problems and doesn't feel so encumbered by society's rules. In ancient China, this was supposed to be the mark of a criminal! In our times, however, I see this shape frequently in successful entrepreneurs and others who've had to figure things out on their own.

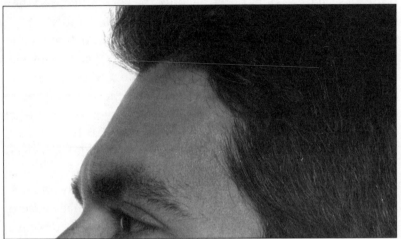

Fig. 28: A forehead that slants back indicates the ability to think of creative ways to make deals.

Under-Eye Area

The under-eye area is one of the places on the face where you can see both physical and emotional aspects reflected. Whenever you see something interesting on someone's face, it's always important to remember that it can have to do with an emotional issue, a health issue, or both. As I described before, Western science is now proving what Chinese medicine has taught and many of us have believed for a long time: Physical imbalances have their genesis in the emotions. The inequity begins with an emotional issue that isn't successfully dealt with, and if it continues for a long enough time, it may manifest physically in some way. Because of this, you may find that both exist at that moment in the life of the

Reading the Water Features

person whose face you're reading. But you can't assume which it is—physical or emotional, or both—without asking questions.

If you're Water, you could very well have natural shadowing around your eyes, especially in this under-eye area. But this is also where you can monitor the physical health of the kidneys in anyone, whether she has this Element or not. In most non-Water people, this area should be smooth, clear, and lightly pink. If dark circles or sunkenness develop where there were none before, it may mean that you've temporarily overused your qi and gotten run down. This is a signal that you need to recharge your batteries, at the very least. It can also be a sign of dehydration, allergies, or even kidney disease, since the kidneys are one of the organs in the body associated with the energy of Water.

If they aren't health related, then dark circles under the eyes can be what are called "unshed tears." They're a sign of suppressed hurt, feelings that haven't yet been released. If the marks are very dark, this is an old, stagnant hurt that has been blocking your system for a long time. If they're reddish in color, this can be a recent hurt that is current in your life.

Even though as Water, you may have dark circles under your eyes naturally, this still isn't something to be completely ignored. As we've learned, this Element feels things deeply, can be easily hurt, and doesn't recover easily. These shadowed under-eye areas are a reflection of the Water temperament, the tendency to feel deeply and hold on to hurts.

Pale circles under the eyes, while not as common, do occur. This can indicate Water deficiency due to an old hurt that's "frozen water," something held so deeply that it's not able to be felt or dealt with. Alternatively, it can mean that you're working too hard, living too frenzied a life, and have "burned up" all your Water. Be aware that both of these issues could be present: You may make the choice of too busy a life simply because it helps you avoid slowing down to look at or feel those deep wounds.

If this coloration is due to feelings being denied, the natural "supply" of Water will eventually become deficient because it's blocked and has stopped moving. If these marks are due to overwork and too hectic a life, the same thing can happen.

85

One of my students had such severe white circles under his eyes that he tried to cover them with makeup each day. He was actually a very Watery man, extremely intuitive, and highly spiritual. However, he wasn't living a lifestyle in line with his Element and actually seemed to be running away from his feelings. This was understandable since he'd endured some extreme traumas earlier in life that he still hadn't dealt with. As a result, he was in denial of most of his emotions.

He was intensely involved in studying kundalini yoga, which includes some extreme breathing techniques such as "Breath of Fire"—a very different energy from Water! He was a single parent of three boys, working too many long hours and having to rush everywhere because his schedule was so packed. None of these are Watery activities. In the end, not only could he not ease his pace, but he actually accelerated it and ended up having a stroke that forced him to change his lifestyle forever.

Puffiness in the under-eye area can be another sign of Water in your personality (Fig. 29). Alternatively, it could mean that your body is over-mineralized, possibly due to drinking a lot of mineral water or eating too much salty food. If not due to a physical cause, swelling in this feature can be an emotional issue rather than a physical one. This is again related to "unshed tears," where feelings are being held instead of allowed to be felt and released.

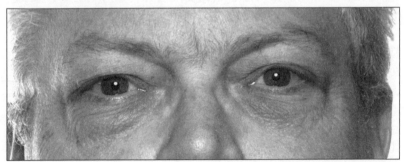

Fig. 29: Puffiness under the eyes is a sign of Water in the personality and possibly of feelings stagnating.

Philtrum

The philtrum is the groove below your nose and above your upper lip, and it's an indicator of creative abilities on many levels. It can help you evaluate details about your physical creativity—your reproductive health, including fertility. If the feature is very well defined or has a deep groove, this is a sign that you're probably very fertile!

If this part of your face is shallow and not well defined, this does *not* mean you won't have children, of course. It just shows that you don't have as much of the primal essence of Water as one of the greatest strengths in your system.

A strong indentation here also indicates a very creative person. Many performers and people involved in the arts have well-defined philtrums. If yours fits this description, you'll most likely be expressing your creativity in other ways in life, even if you never have children. There are many avenues to make use of your fertility.

The Chinese believed that a long, well-defined philtrum was a sign that you'd live a long and healthy life. This still has to do with the issue of reproductive health: If you were highly fertile, you'd have many children, meaning that you'd be well taken care of in your old age, and therefore live a long and happy life! However, there may be something more to this belief, if you look at the essence of Water. This Element has a lot to do with your inherent life force and the will to live. If you have strong signs of Water on your face, it may be that you have the strength of will to be able to survive what others could not.

It's not uncommon to see markings within the groove of the philtrum. This can be a general sign that there is or has been a problem with the physical health of the reproductive system. With men, it can mean issues with the prostate or testes; in women it could be any of the reproductive organs. For example, it might be a sign that there was surgery on the reproductive system. As always, though, markings on a feature may have to do with an emotional issue. In this case, it could mean a difficult experience around getting pregnant or having babies, or it might indicate problems involving your creative process rather than your physical fertility.

A horizontal line across a woman's philtrum (Fig. 30) usually shows that she has lost a child through miscarriage, abortion, or death after birth. Or it could mean that she's had a hysterectomy or other surgery on her reproductive system or experienced a difficult menopause. I rarely see this line in men who have lost a child because it didn't affect their physical bodies. Instead this is usually marked on their face at the age they experienced the trauma.

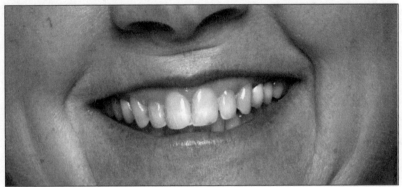

Fig. 30: A horizontal line through the philtrum usually indicates loss of a child or reproductive-health issues.

A vertical line down this feature can mean that there's a stressful issue around one or more of your children and that has therefore marked your face. Again, it can instead be a reflection of a problem with personal creativity and the products of those endeavors.

The philtrum also marks an important transition in life that occurs at age 50. But even here, it still has a lot to do with fertility and creativity issues. If you're a woman, this is a time in life when you begin to transform your reproductive energy into a new expression. It's often a time of beginning menopause and becoming freed from that aspect of your biology. You can now move into manifesting your creativity in an entirely new way, perhaps finally having time to let this side of your personality emerge. For men, it's often the beginning of a new kind of creative urge as well, examining your life and feeling the desire to express yourself in a more fulfilling way.

Chin

The chin is the indicator of the level of willpower, determination, and tenacity you have. The stronger the chin in comparison to the rest of the features on your face, the more Watery fortitude you have. It also represents the physical health of the bladder.

A strong chin (Fig. 31) indicates a strong will, but that also means a stubborn nature. However, this can often be a positive quality in the appropriate situations!

Fig. 31: A strong chin represents a strong will.

If your boss has a prominent chin, this could be why she has attained such a high position in the first place. If your child's chin sticks out, it may be a struggle for you as the parent, but you can rest assured that in adult life this is one person who won't be pushed around.

A weak chin or one that has markings such as wrinkles, scarring, or dimpling is often a sign of Water deficiency in willpower (Fig. 32). If you have such indicators, they may be a sign that you've had to deal with a lot of fear in your life or had to use a lot of your willpower and thus depleted your Water. This can translate into difficulty standing up for yourself; or it can lead you to

overcompensate so that you're overly negative or have trouble forgiving in an attempt to protect yourself.

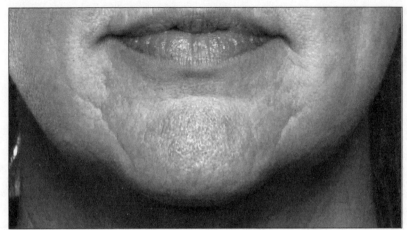

Fig. 32: Markings on the chin may reflect having had to use up too much willpower.

I remember an interview with actress Carol Burnett where she talked about her plastic surgery for an implant to give her a stronger chin. She said that she was surprised to discover that after the surgery, she felt as though she could stand up for herself for the first time in her life. This is totally in line with what face reading teaches us. She'd experienced a traumatic childhood with alcoholic parents and may well have had to use a great force of will just to survive emotionally. As an adult, changing her chin enhanced her Water qi and helped her gain the ability to be stubborn!

One specific kind of "weak" chin is a receding chin (Fig. 33), which is a sign of having been oppressed or dominated in the past, usually during childhood. This can have a major impact on your overall experience of life. Sometimes it can result in your having a pessimistic outlook on life, being passive, and giving up easily. You might even revert to more childish behavior under pressure, to the point of acting in emotionally immature ways; severe stress could send you into a state of feeling childlike and helpless. The pattern of not being allowed to stand up for yourself when you were little creates an inner powerlessness that continues in adult life. A small subset of people with receding chins will tend to see everyone through the filter of being oppressed and live like victims—whining, complaining, and making everyone else miserable.

But be careful not to make quick assumptions. If you have a receding chin, you may instead end up fighting for the underdog and not being weak or powerless at all. This is because you know what it's like to be mistreated, and you make it your mission to fight to help those who are going through what you did.

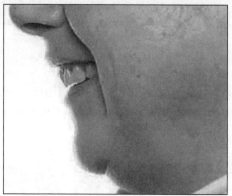

Fig. 33: A receding chin usually means oppression early in life.

A cleft chin is often referred to as the sign of the performer (Fig. 34). It indicates a strong desire for attention and appreciation, but this doesn't mean you're egotistical or vain if you have this marking. However, it *does* show that you genuinely need acknowledgment and attention. If you have a job where you work behind the scenes, it's essential that at some point you're brought out to be given the appreciation you so dearly need. If this doesn't happen, you'll be unhappy but may not know why.

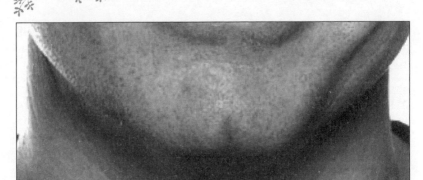

Fig. 34: A cleft chin shows a need for attention.

A chin that's pointed (Fig. 35) shows a tendency to be indecisive or more easily influenced by others or by your emotions. You may make a decision but then waver when a friend offers a different opinion, or you may change your mind too easily according to your mood.

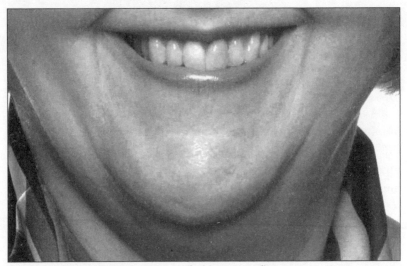

Fig. 35: A pointed chin can mean an indecisive personality.

Another mark of strong Water, a large chin (Fig. 36) usually indicates a highly intuitive nature and intense willpower. The Chinese also consider it a sign of long life, as potent Water equals a vigorous will to live.

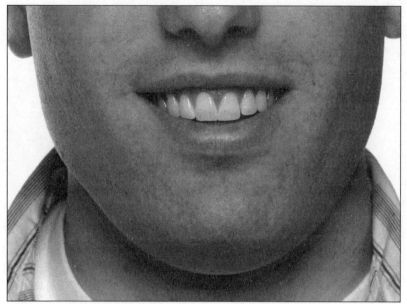

Fig. 36: A large chin represents strong intuition and tenacity.

Anytime there's an added roundness to a feature, it means some added kindness and tact. A rounded chin (Fig. 37) is a sign that even if you have a large "stubborn" chin, you'll express your willfulness with diplomacy!

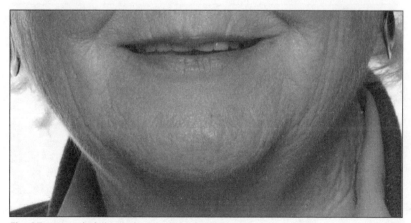

Fig. 37: A rounded chin indicates extra personal warmth.

Any feature with a squared-off shape indicates added practicality. A squared chin (Fig. 38) means that you have an extra supply of common sense and an ability to approach things in a logical way.

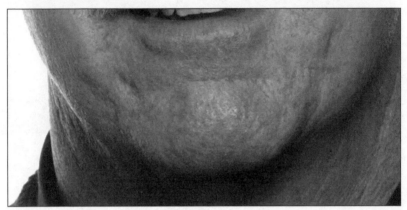

Fig. 38: A square chin is a sign of practicality.

A double chin (Fig. 39) is sometimes considered to be a sign that you can hold more than one opinion or that you're able to see all sides of a problem and consider everyone's viewpoint. The Chinese also believe that this feature means comfort in your old age!

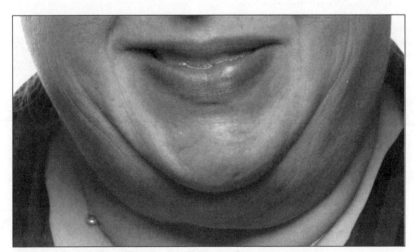

Fig. 39: A double chin indicates a less judgmental nature.

Water: Who Are You? What Is Your Calling?

Who are you, and how can you fall in love with who you really are? How can you clear the way for your true calling to emerge? You must first allow your Water essence to flourish in order to manifest your purpose in the world. If this is your Element, your true nature is one that carries within it a deep wisdom and a connection to the primal, powerful mysteries of life. The intense feelings others may try to suppress or deny are vitally present in your system, and you should allow them as a source of great nourishment for yourself and a way to support others. Summon and acknowledge your courage to experience these emotions and still be able to speak about them. Allow the tears to come, then bless them for showing that you can have such a depth of feeling.

Find ways to use your greatest strengths: your intuition, creativity, and determination. Empower yourself by forming a life that has space for your need to be free and independent. Don't suppress fear when it arises—instead, feel it and let it go. Keep a dream journal because dreams are your powerful messengers. Accept your nonlinear way of being, and cultivate your spirituality and sensuality. Give yourself regular spaces of time to float, muse, and submerge yourself in the rich seas of your Watery soul. When your Water qi is flowing, life will come into balance, and you can encounter new possibilities beyond your wildest dreams.

Chapter 7

WOOD—TO DO

In this chapter, I'll introduce the basics of the Wood Element, and you'll learn how to identify it. To begin, here's a quick-reference list of Wood characteristics:

- **Energy:** upward moving, pushing, active, morning, spring, childhood

- **Qualities:** optimistic, enthusiastic, active, humanitarian, confident, angry, frustrated, impulsive, reactive, direct, perceptive, practical, logical, organized, decisive, judgmental, curious, eager to learn, competitive, pushy, driven, rebellious, disciplined

- **Major features:** brow bone, eyebrows, temples, jaw

- **Organs:** liver, gallbladder

- **Sense organ:** Eyes

What to Look for

You don't need to have *all* of the following aspects for this Element to play a strong role in your life—any of these will indicate that it's a factor in your personality. The more of them you possess, the more Wood there is in your nature:

- Thick, strong eyebrows
- Protruding brow bone
- Indented temples
- Prominent or well-defined jaw
- Tall and lanky body type—or short and compact
- Greenish-brown undertone to complexion

Fig. 40: Wood Face

Fig. 41: Wood Face

How do you know if the Wood Element is a major part of your personality? You look for your strongest features—what's most noticeable on your face. You may not have all or even many of the kinds of features listed above, but if one of the first things you notice is your prominent jaw or strong eyebrows, you have this energy in your makeup. The more Wood features you have, the more Wood you have in your personality.

This is a unique Element in that it has two very different body types associated with it. If you're a typical Wood person, you might be tall and lanky like a basketball player or a short, compact dynamo similar to a gymnast—in other words, either a "tree" or a "shrub"! Your eyebrows may be strong and your jaw well defined. You could have sinewy muscles and a natural tension in your body so that even when you're relaxed, you tend to hold your hand in a fist. You may have a brown complexion with a slight greenish undertone and indented temples. If you have all of these characteristics, which is rare, you'll know that you are a very Woody person!

Well-known faces that show the Wood Element include: Hilary Swank, Brad Pitt, Katie Couric, Arnold Schwarzenegger, Maria Shriver, and Tom Cruise.

Wood Energy and Power

The energy of this Element is forceful and dynamic. It's the little child running and shouting, the immense power of the trees pushing their way skyward, and the bright optimism of a brand-new day.

The power of Wood is in transforming energy into matter. It takes the formless force of Water and makes it manifest in the world, as new beginnings and growth. This Element has to do with the transition the baby makes as it moves from being merged with its mother into being born and existing as a separate presence in the world. It's about establishing individuality, the process of defining yourself as the unique spirit you are. And so Wood also gives definition to things—focusing, planning, creating structure, and putting ideas into action.

Like all new life, Wood energy is enthusiastic and interested in everything. It's the endless animation of a child who's going at life with gusto, a bright spirit that's into something new every few minutes. There's also a tension present, similar to what you see in children's bodies, so alert and aroused in this fascinating new world that every muscle is alive and at attention. But ideally, this quality is balanced by flexibility, as is required when one is growing. Just as the tree is deeply rooted in the ground and its branches sway in the breeze, so can you hold firmly to your convictions but also be able to adjust when conditions require you to do so.

This Element is about *doing*, putting creative ideas into action, and so the verb for Wood is "to do." If you're a Wood person, you carry that vitality, that pushing forward, in every cell of your being.

The Personality of Wood

The energy of this Element is illustrated by the force of the plant bursting through the ground in the spring, the baby pushing through the birth canal, and the drive to take action. It's the force that helps us go out into the world and work to make something of ourselves. While Water is persistent and determined, Wood is focused and intense, pushing against all obstacles in its path.

If you're Wood, your major strengths are your optimism, enthusiasm, and urge to go out and change the world for the better. You may be the humanitarian who fights for a cause, breaking up the old to make way for the new. Or you may have the personality of the pioneer, always initiating fresh ideas, ever enthusiastic and curious to learn new things and push forward. Most of all, you're about *doing,* and you love to be active—with exercise, work, movement of any sort, and even intellectually with a lot of interests or new ideas.

One of my students with a lot of Wood Element in his face had a job that required a long commute. He drove 90 minutes to work in the morning and back again each night, but he wasn't frustrated by all that time in the car. He kept a set of small barbells under his seat so he could drive with one hand and exercise with the other!

In fact, if these people can't be active, they'll become depressed. This is actually a common imbalance in this Element due to rage turned inward; anger toward the self or others is the issue for Wood. Just as Water will tend to go into the emotion of fear, the challenge here is anger or frustration. If you're Wood, you may become so frustrated when you're stressed that you'll explode into an outburst of irritation or even fury—or you might express it by being impulsive and making a too-sudden decision.

Under pressure, Wood needs to blow off steam. A healthy member of this group will make a balanced choice on how to do so, such as working with tools, digging in the garden, or going out jogging. If this energy goes out of balance, you'll shout at your partner to get it out of your system or storm out of a meeting.

In looking at how just the first two Elements, Water and Wood, approach life, you can already begin to see the problems that can

occur when people of two different energies try to coexist. I once consulted with parents who were very worried about their child. They were both highly Wood, but their daughter was Water. They were up at 6 A.M. on the weekends, pulling on their hiking boots and ready to head for the hills; it frustrated them that it was such a problem to even pry their daughter from her bed, let alone get her out the door for a strenuous morning excursion. Of course, as Water, she wanted to linger as long as possible in that beautiful half-dream state of slowly wakening. Her favorite activity for the morning would be lying in bed reading or drawing, not conquering nature. And once out and about, she'd want to slowly explore as she walked rather than march forward through the brush.

Here was a child who was already being judged and absorbing information that something was wrong with her. This happened to most of us in early life, being appraised through the filter of our family's personalities. I was thrilled to have the opportunity to see the grown-ups' faces light up with understanding as we talked about Wood and Water. Their blame disappeared, and in the end, they were able to find ways to nurture the wonderful person she was. What a gift to parents face reading can be!

If you're Wood, you can find satisfaction in business and athletics because you're competitive and seek challenges. Attorneys often have a lot of Wood in their personalities, which comes out in their debating skills. One friend commented to me that these people love to argue . . . only they call it a "discussion"! If you find that a fight energizes you, then you probably have some of this Element. If it exhausts or upsets you, however, it's likely you don't have much Wood in your nature.

If you're not in a competitive career, you'll probably enjoy working out in nature or with tools. If your profession isn't typically Wood, then it's likely you'll feel the need to be active in your free time in order to satisfy that Elemental urge. You aren't the one who lingers in bed on Sunday mornings; you're either working against a deadline or out rock climbing, loving the feeling of risk and being pushed to the breaking point.

But Wood is also practical and sensible and appreciates organization. You hate to fuss or fiddle with things: You'll get rid of the spare change from your pockets the moment you get home, and you'll probably never pull out a stack of coupons at the grocery store. This Element loves to create systems and structure and delights in organizing and planning projects. In work or conversation, you're straightforward and to the point. Sometimes you may even stare too intensely or directly as you speak to someone and thus make him uncomfortable. And if the other person wanders in conversation, your impatience will rise. You may not be able to resist tapping your foot and finally interrupting to tell him to cut to the chase.

Just as Wood is associated with the new plant emerging in the spring, one of your greatest strengths is the ability to come up with new ways to do things and then plan out a structure for the project to happen. But while you're wonderful at initiating things and creating systems for their development, you're not always good at follow-through. Because of this, it's best that you work in conjunction with someone who can tend to the details of your big ideas. Like all of us, you should be supported in your strengths as much as possible and not forced to be something you aren't.

Wood is resilient and not overly sensitive. This is a wonderful quality that lets you get things done in life and not be bogged down with time spent processing feelings, as Water will tend to do. Words that would pierce a Water person's heart may roll right off your back. In fact, because it's your nature to be direct and to the point, others might perceive you as blunt or even tactless; you could even be seen as insensitive sometimes and not realize it. The unfortunate result can be that you become reactive to the hurt feelings of others and end up in an argument—which may come pretty naturally to you!

Wood Style

— **Clothing:** Wood values logic and common sense. You're all about moving forward without obstacles, so if this is your Element, your choices in clothes fit these needs. Athletic, outdoorsy, or preppy clothing is common, often in denim, khaki, or shades of green. Above all, practical clothes are what you'll love. You want to be active, so you need apparel that doesn't restrict motion. You won't wear anything that you have to fuss with. If you're a Wood woman, you don't choose bows, lace, or frilly details; and you'll fill your closet with running shoes, hiking boots, or sensible shoes. You'll disdain high heels and avoid them if at all possible. If you have to wear them, they won't be pointy stilettos, but low or chunky versions with squared-off toes.

Hairstyles for both men and women will be extremely easy to care for. Because Wood hates to fuss, we'll never see you maintaining an elaborate coiffure. Most likely your hair is short and easy to care for or long and tucked behind your ears.

— **Home:** The homes of this Element often have more of a masculine or rustic décor. Ralph Lauren–style furnishings are in character, as is anything that has the ambience of a hunting lodge or log cabin. You may put lots of actual wood in the space, using it for most of the furniture, wall paneling, or tall vertical bookcases that evoke the shape of trees. There may be plants (as long as they don't require complicated care), or your view will be of trees. Artwork will tend to be nature images, not abstracts. Because of your love for structure, your books may be arranged alphabetically by author, and your tax records logically filed. You'll find little clutter in Wood homes, and in fact, if you ever want to hire a clutter-clearing consultant, I suggest someone from this Element!

— **Movement:** Almost any exercise is great because you need to keep active. Running, mountain biking, backpacking, strength training, and competitive and team sports are all supportive of Wood vibrations. And anytime your energy is low, the best place for you to revitalize yourself is out in nature. A brisk walk through the trees will do much more for you than a nap.

— **Profession:** Because Wood loves logic and a good argument, you may be drawn to the field of law. The profession not only gives you the opportunity to argue and debate, but it also fulfills your need to change the world for the better. This desire makes you well

equipped to succeed in politics or social activism as well. Or you could be the philanthropist or humanitarian, using your money, time, and energy for good in the world.

Your high level of competitiveness and drive, as well as your appreciation for structure, helps you excel in business, professional sports, or law enforcement. Working with tools or wood, or building things is also great for this Element, so fields such as carpentry and construction are excellent. Other careers involve systems and organization, such as architecture, urban planning, and especially landscape design because it will bring you outdoors, which is very nourishing for Wood. In fact, any work that can be done outside is supportive of your energy. And due to your enthusiasm for learning, no matter what profession you end up in, you'll always be a lifelong student.

Perhaps you've recognized yourself or a friend in the descriptions above, and it may have given you new insights and awareness. But you may feel that while you see *some* Wood, it doesn't completely describe you or your friend. Remember that while we all have some of each of the five Elements in our personalities, usually one or two are emphasized. Some people even have four of the Elements strongly in their faces and are weak in only one. So it may be as you read further, you can identify a second, third, or even fourth category that gives you a complete understanding of who you are inside.

But even if you don't find Wood features emphasized in your face, you still have eyebrows, a jaw, and temples! In the next chapter, we'll examine each of these features individually and learn what they can tell us in more detail about how this Element manifests in your inherent spirit.

Chapter 8

READING THE WOOD FEATURES

As I've mentioned, in addition to giving the entire face a certain look, each Element corresponds with specific facial features. In this chapter, you'll learn how to gain even more insight into the Wood Element from each of these body parts.

Eyebrows

The strongest facial indicators of this Element are the eyebrows. If yours are thick, bushy, or long, you have strong Wood qi and the potential for drive, confidence, and ambition—as well as impatience, frustration, and anger. This doesn't mean that if you fit this description you're an angry person! Some people with this type of feature rarely exhibit this emotion, probably because they already feel so confident in their power that they don't have to go there.

But overall, if you have thick eyebrows, you'll have these tendencies. You may not get frequently lost in anger, but you may be easily frustrated, reactive, or impulsive when stressed. You'll want to push ahead in projects or may find it hard to resist the urge to blast someone who you feel is standing in the way of getting things done.

The more prominent this feature is, the more drive and confidence you have, and the more you'll probably want to be the one in charge. This can be an incredibly positive ability, as you can even take the lead in difficult situations. However, extremely bushy eyebrows can indicate a domineering temperament, which can negatively impact relationships. Very thick brows that join in the center, sometimes called a "unibrow," are a sign of enormous Wood energy, and if you have this, you may have to work very hard to control your anger. This is one of the times that I do recommend plucking, because others will subconsciously feel threatened if you don't.

Your eyebrows also indicate the health of your liver, the organ that processes the toxins in your body. Strong eyebrows show vigorous liver qi and therefore the ability to deal more successfully with toxic substances such as alcohol, as well as powerful emotions like anger.

Thick eyebrows tend to be an issue for women in our culture because they're not usually considered fashionable. So many women pluck them, sometimes making them very thin. It's interesting that eyebrows are a sign of the level of drive, confidence, aggression, and anger, which are all considered "masculine" attributes in our current times. So women are basically sending this message to the world: "Don't worry—I'm not a threat!"

Because the strength of the eyebrows directly relates to the level of overall assertiveness and confidence someone feels, I do advise all women, regardless of whether they have Wood Element, to not pluck too severely. You don't want to feel disempowered! Many of my female clients had already done so for such a long time, however, that the hairs stopped growing back. In these cases, I do find that low self-confidence can be a major problem. If this has happened to you, one solution is to use makeup to draw in more of your eyebrows, as any change to the face will have a corresponding effect on the emotions. But I find it even more valuable for you to consciously work on your issues around feeling assertive and confident. Interestingly, I've seen many instances when someone did begin nurturing these feelings, and her eyebrows started growing in thicker!

Women who tweeze their brows into pencil-thin lines or who have eliminated them completely in order to replace them with a very narrow drawn-on eyebrow can actually have a significant problem with anger. They may be unconsciously trying to hide— even from themselves—how much rage they actually have. They're often living in denial of their true feelings. Their healthy Wood energy is being suppressed, and it shows in their eyebrows.

Long brows are a sign of extra Wood and are often considered a sign of the ability to maintain a lot of friendships (Fig. 42). Again, the ability to deal with "toxic information" comes into play. You'll be able to handle friends' different personalities much more easily than someone who doesn't have this kind of vitality.

Of course, if your brows are short, you'll certainly have friends, too! But it's likely you'll exhibit the need to be less involved in their lives in some way, unless there are other aspects of your face that modify this tendency. Overall, if you have short eyebrows, you may be less likely to ask for help, because doing so would require you to be available to return the favor, and you aren't very comfortable having to cope with others' problems.

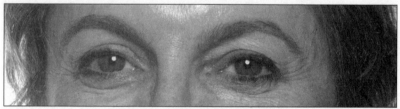

Fig. 42: Long eyebrows are a sign of the ability to maintain many friendships.

How far apart or close together your eyebrows grow tells you how well you "play with others." If they're far apart in the middle—in other words, if there is a wide space between them (Fig. 43)—you're a person who can get along well with a broad range of personalities. Because of this, you can be successful working on teams or in the corporate world.

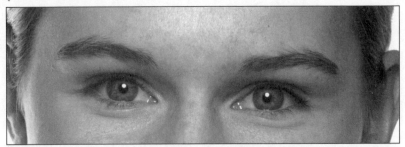

Fig. 43: A wide space between the eyebrows indicates the ability to deal with a broad range of personalities.

If your eyebrows come together with just a narrow space between them (Fig. 44), you'll be less comfortable in a large organization where you have to cope with many different kinds of personalities. Even having a supervisor can be uncomfortable, as you'll tend to feel micromanaged. It's best to find a position where you have a lot of independence and privacy, or start your own business and work for yourself.

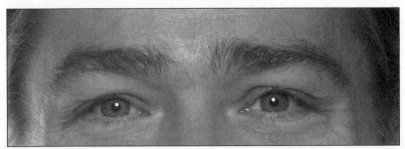

Fig. 44: A narrow space between the eyebrows shows a greater need for working independently.

Another telling piece of information the inner ends of the eyebrows can offer is how harshly you judge yourself. If the points come down quite close to the inner corners of your eyes (Fig. 45), this is an indication that you're hard on yourself. You'll hold the bar for your accomplishments quite high and tend to beat yourself up if you can't reach your goals in the ways you feel you should.

If the inner ends of your eyebrows are higher than the outer ones, the opposite is true: You'll be more critical of others than yourself. Senator Joseph McCarthy, who instigated the Communist "witch hunt" back in the 1950s, had eyebrows like this. He was certainly an extreme example of this personality trait—it usually shows up in a much less dramatic way in most people's lives!

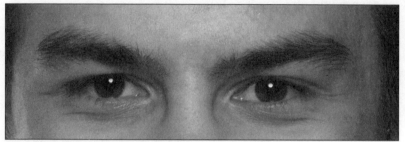

Fig. 45: The inner ends of the eyebrows here show a tendency toward self-criticism.

If your eyebrows are low and close to the eye overall (Fig. 46), you'll probably have high expectations for both yourself and everyone else, and may have difficulty separating your own sense of worth from how others perform. Similar to a sports coach, you'll have a tendency to be overinvolved in whether your "team" (in any sense of the word) wins or loses.

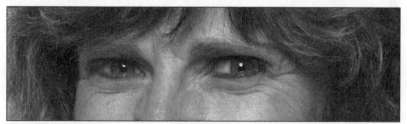

Fig. 46: Eyebrows close to the eyes reflect the need to stay closely involved with others.

While this can be a great challenge, it also has a positive side. Author Wayne Dyer appears to be a good example of how this quality can be used successfully. I was having dinner with a colleague and was describing how Wayne has these kind of eyebrows. My friend exclaimed that he knew Wayne and felt that one of his great strengths in helping people was that he never gave up on them. If he took your hand, he'd stay with you for the long haul and make sure that you made it to your personal finish line. So this ability to be fully involved can definitely be a wonderful asset.

The shape of the eyebrows also reveals other important information. Curves tell the world that you have a pleasant personality and care about others' feelings. In any negotiations, you'll strive for a win-win outcome (Fig. 47).

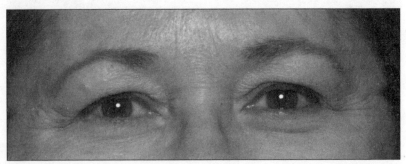

Fig. 47: Curved eyebrows reveal a pleasing nature.

Strong curves are called "Concubine's Eyebrows." In ancient China, a concubine would shave off her brows and draw in exaggerated curves to communicate that her only desire was to please. In fact, these are considered to be the sign of a manipulator who's hiding her true intentions and handling things indirectly.

If your eyebrows are more of a straight line than a curve (Fig. 48), you'll take your time in sizing up a situation and not be reactive. You'll evaluate things more logically and weigh your choices carefully. You may also be seen as someone who's rather skeptical, not buying into every story that comes your way. However, once you make a decision, you won't want to let anything stand in your way!

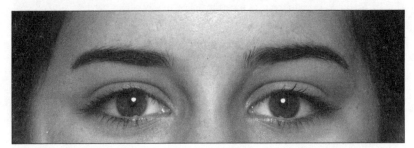

Fig. 48: Eyebrows in a straight line show the ability to evaluate a situation logically.

If your eyebrows are arched and have a peak (Fig. 49), you like action. You can make fast decisions—possibly too hasty at times. You also may be more reactive emotionally, which might not always serve you well. In this case, your more deliberate-minded friends are great assets, so share your ideas with them before you make a final choice.

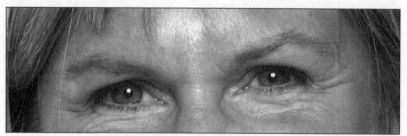

Fig. 49: Arched eyebrows show the potential to leap into action.

If your eyebrows go straight up (Fig. 50), you will hit the ground running. You can instantly leap into action, but you may have to endure the consequences of getting carried away by your emotions. In this case, it would serve you well to have a trusted friend who's grounded and practical to help slow you down!

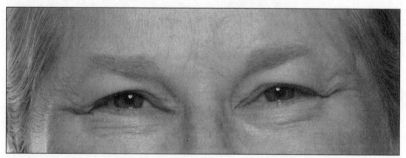

Fig. 50: Eyebrows that slant up reveal the ability to react instantly.

Again, a reminder: You can't make an accurate judgment about an entire personality based on one feature. Each body part we're talking about is a single aspect of your entire nature, something to be noticed but taken into consideration with the rest of your face in order to get a complete picture of who you truly are.

Brow Bone

The brow bone (Fig. 51) is naturally more prominent in a man's face than a woman's because it correlates to levels of testosterone. This is the feature that shows how much you need to be in control, dominant, and in charge. The larger it is, the greater the desire. A big, protruding brow bone in either gender is a sign of someone who probably has issues with authority and doesn't like being told what to do. If you're in a relationship with someone who looks like this, you may find that he tends to perceive even the slightest request as an order. You might say, "Could you please pass the salt?" But he's likely to hear, "Do what I say, *now!*" This isn't an easy situation in any relationship, so it's important to try to stay conscious of this Wood challenge and the difficulties it can create.

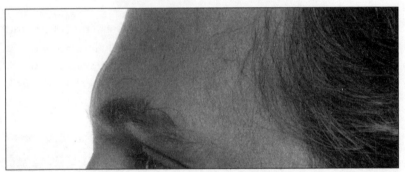

Fig. 51: The brow bone shows how strongly you need to be in charge.

But while a protruding brow doesn't bode well for personal relationships, it does have a positive connotation. Just as it shows the desire to be in charge, it also represents the enormous potential to be a powerful leader.

"Seat of the Stamp"

In the center of the brow bone, the area between the eyebrows is called the "Seat of the Stamp" or "Father's Blessing" (Fig. 52). When officials in ancient China signed documents, they applied a "chop" or stamp that had their insignia carved into it, which was a sign of official approval. The more important the position a man held, the bigger the stamp he used. Because the brow bone is such a sign of power in the face, the size and condition of the center brow was considered a way to foretell one's potential for might and success. The more space there was on that part of the face, the larger the stamp that could be applied. So the bigger this area is for you, the more likelihood there is of power and authority manifesting in your life.

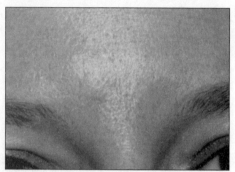

Fig. 52: The Seat of the Stamp is located on the brow bone between the eyebrows.

But underlying this meaning is also another sense of "Father's Blessing"—receiving validation of your worth and potency as a person from the one who holds the most authority in your young life. This is usually your father (or whoever held that position in your family). If you're loved and supported by this person, you'll grow up feeling able and strong; your power has been blessed. If you didn't receive this kind of treatment, it's likely that you'll have issues around your sense of personal authority. This will mark your face in the Seat of the Stamp.

Ideally, this feature should be broad, smooth, and slightly protruding with no indentations, lines, or discolorations. This indicates Wood in balance, showing no contention with authority or problems with anger or frustration. But this Element is out of balance quite a bit in our Western society as a whole, so many

people have markings in this area of the face. The most common are two small vertical lines (Fig. 53). These can indicate a tendency toward anger or frustration—or at least impatience or irritability. Purposely make a "mad" face and most likely you'll immediately press your eyebrows together and create lines between them. Many repetitions of this expression, even subtly, over a long period of time will carve these marks into your face.

The other cause of these lines has less to do with specific negative emotions and more to do with the essence of Wood energy—that of inner tension. If you intensely concentrate as you work, you'll probably be making a frown that creates those marks as well. All people in this Element will have a tendency to develop them, and it's an easy way to spot Wood as a major part of someone's nature.

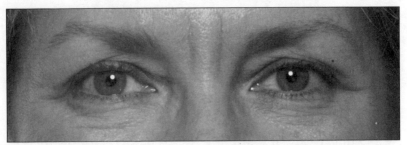

Fig. 53: Two vertical lines between the eyebrows show Wood emotions and/or tension.

It's possible to have these lines show up temporarily while you're dealing with a phase of life that's frustrating to you or that's making you work very hard. As you move beyond this stressful time, if you haven't made a new habit of those emotions and can instead let them go, the wrinkles will fade or disappear.

In every lecture and class, the question of cosmetic surgery comes up. Students ask about Botox treatments and other types of manipulation to change the face. It might seem logical that taking those vertical lines away from your brow would help give you an opportunity to eliminate issues of anger, frustration, or too much tension and effort held in your system, giving you a clean slate. But the emotions are still felt inside your body, so you'll continue to try to express them physically in some way. And when the Botox wears off, the wrinkles will return. Nothing has shifted inside, which is where the only sustainable change can happen.

Any plastic surgery on wrinkles formed by a repeated facial expression actually does give you a window to work on the issues that have been causing that expression, which in turn creates the lines. This opportunity is said to usually last from three to five years at most. If you don't make the internal changes, the wrinkles simply return, as you stay in that same pattern of emotion. I recently talked to a woman who'd had a complete face-lift only 18 months before, and all the wrinkles had already returned!

When cosmetic "queen" Estée Lauder died, there was a lengthy obituary in the newspaper. In it, she was quoted as saying that there's one time in each woman's life when she's certain to be beautiful: That's her wedding day, because on that day she will take great care with her makeup. When I read that, I was appalled. A woman is beautiful when she gets married not because of her makeup, but because she's in love! The goal of my work is to help you cultivate and enhance that inner glow for yourself and others. If you're radiating love, you'll be seen by others as beautiful, whether you have wrinkles, no makeup, or a big nose—and certainly without having to cut your face.

"Hanging Needle"

A small, shallow single line down the middle of the Seat of the Stamp is called a "Hanging Needle" (Fig. 54). When you see this in your face, it indicates an issue with your personal power. It can mean that you didn't feel fully empowered by your dominant parent or weren't allowed to show your anger earlier in life. It could be that you were ruled by a parent or authority figure who had anger issues. If your father was frequently absent or not emotionally available to you as a child, this could also cause the mark.

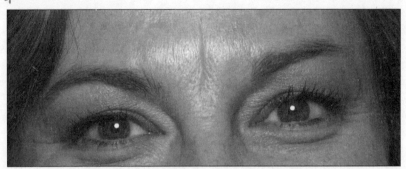

Fig. 54: A shallow line between the eyebrows is a Hanging Needle.

A Hanging Needle indicates that you may not feel very assertive as you move through life. You may find it a challenge to keep others from taking advantage of you or struggle to summon the necessary drive for finding full success in life. With this wrinkle, there's a block to being able move into your power.

"Hanging Blade"

A deeper single line through the middle of the Seat of the Stamp is referred to as a "Hanging Blade" (Fig. 55). This more significant marking gives a stronger emphasis to the same influence as a Hanging Needle. There may be estrangement from your father or whoever was the authority figure in your childhood; there will be a corresponding estrangement from your yang side, your own sense of personal power. This wrinkle is often a sign that your dominant parent had severe anger problems or was completely absent emotionally or physically. Because of this, you can feel tremendous suppressed rage or drive. You may have problems with frustration, impatience, reactivity, or anger in your life—there's a major block to your Wood qi that needs to be resolved.

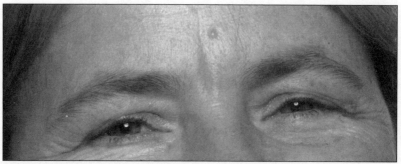

Fig. 55: A deep line between the eyebrows is a Hanging Blade.

With both the Hanging Needle and Hanging Blade, the belief is that at some point in your life, the needle or blade will "drop" and stop your forward progress until the issue is dealt with. If you aren't accessing your power or fully using your potential, you can only go so far in life. Interestingly, I do find that many people who have these markings are on spiritual paths. They're the ones who on some level have realized that they need to release the blockage to activate their unused power and are doing the work necessary to move through these issues.

Wood Element is associated with vision. Interestingly, the Seat of the Stamp is also considered the entrance to the "third eye," the home of your intuitive vision, and clearing obstructions here can have a deep influence on your ability to "see" with your inner eye.

Three or more vertical lines in this area are actually a positive sign because they're judged to be an indication that you have been working on any issues of anger or tension, and as a result have grown personally as well.

Discolorations in the Seat of the Stamp are also meaningful. Dark areas indicate stagnation, which can be an issue with the health of your liver, with anger, or both. Shadows here indicate an old, long-term problem. Redness signifies a current situation, often repressed rage. Sometimes the flush appears in your face only when you're talking about the person who is stimulating that emotion—often your father, boss, and/or spouse!

However, any marking on your face can also have to do with the age it relates to. (If you recall the Facial Maps on pages 42 and 43, each year of your life has a corresponding point on your face.) The Seat of the Stamp is at the approximate age of 28 or 29. This is an important transition point in life, and a marking can indicate that something important did (or will) happen.

Temples

The sides of the forehead or temples are also a Wood feature. There's one main thing to look for here. If the temples look indented or slightly concave (Fig. 56), this indicates a tendency toward compulsive or addictive behavior. This is an emphasis of Wood Element's natural inner tension. I read an interview once with the director of a new addiction-treatment center, in which he was quoted as saying: "Addicts are never relaxed in their own skin." This is an excellent description of what Wood—and especially indented temples—represents.

This isn't to say that if you have such features then you're a drug addict! Any compulsive tendencies can show up in a range of ways. You may have a "workaholic" personality, so driven that you're at the job long hours and rarely take a day off, or you may be easily hooked on exercise. I had one client with highly indented temples who had a compulsion about television. He traveled frequently for his sales job and found that instead of working in his hotel room, he couldn't resist the pull of the large TV that dominated the space. Closing the cabinet doors to hide it wasn't enough, but he finally solved his problem by disciplining himself to immediately remove the batteries from the remote control as soon as he checked in, hiding them under the mattress! In fact, Wood does have great powers of discipline and can deal with any urges successfully by channeling them into healthy activities.

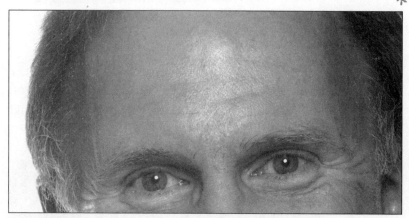

Fig. 56: Indented temples reveal a tendency toward compulsive behavior of some sort.

Indented temples also indicate a craving for the state of consciousness that's induced by the addiction. This altered perception can be achieved in many different ways, with drugs, alcohol, compulsive work, exercise, or sex being some of the most common. But this state can also be one that creates opportunities for growth and transcendence when it's reached through another avenue: spirituality. And so indented temples can indicate a highly spiritual person, someone who has addictive tendencies, or both. Often people involved in meditation or a faith tradition first experienced a similar altered state with drugs but were able to find a healthier and more productive method of achieving an even higher and sustainable level of consciousness. This may be part of the reason for the success of Alcoholics Anonymous. It channels an addict's desire for that altered state from alcohol into accessing it through spirituality.

Very occasionally, you may spot someone with temples that have subtle diagonal lines extending down toward the face. This is a mark that this person will go or has gone through some form of "dark night of the soul," a time of deep personal and spiritual work that can result in significant transformation.

Temples that are full or even plump are a sign of someone who's more content in the present moment, who enjoys the pleasures of life on Earth. He or she probably doesn't feel a driving urge toward achieving altered states.

Jaw

After the eyebrows, the jaw is the best indicator of the level of Wood in your personality. This feature is called "The Roots of the Tree." A tree with strong roots can't be pushed over, and if you have a prominent jaw (Fig. 57), you'll tend to have a strong belief system and won't be easily swayed.

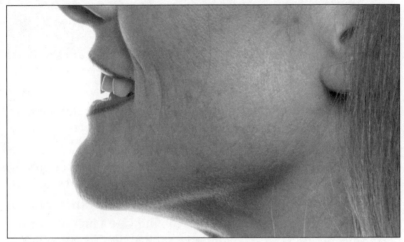

Fig. 57: A strong jaw means strong convictions.

I find that politicians with strong jaws are often the ones who win elections because people subconsciously feel safe and protected by someone they feel will stand up for them. However, if you have this appearance, there's a chance that you're too judgmental of others, which can potentially interfere in relationships.

If your jaw is so large that it dominates your face, it can mean that you're too forceful in your opinions. You can be severely judgmental, telling others what to do—whether they want to hear it or not! At the extreme is someone who tries to get everyone to think as he does. The stereotype of this is the military man with a set jaw and the attitude of "my country, right or wrong." This kind of person can be domineering and controlling, and if there are no other features that diminish this effect, he can be very difficult to relate to.

A narrow jaw (Fig. 58) shows that you aren't as set in your ways. You're adaptable and open-minded. However, you may actually be swayed by your emotions or easily influenced by persuasive people. If the roots of the tree are shallow, it could fall in the wind. At the extreme, this could mean that you're inclined to align yourself with whomever you think will benefit you the most, which can affect your reputation with others.

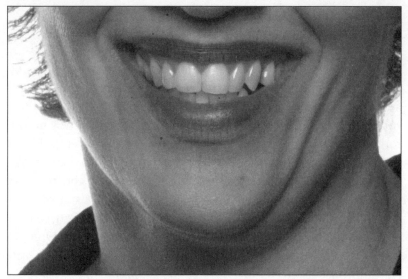

Fig. 58: A narrow jaw reflects a more adaptable nature.

Stature

Wood has two very distinct body types associated with it: the tall, lanky "tree" or stereotypical basketball player; and the short and compact "shrub" or gymnast type. The latter seems to be a condensed form of the strong energy that's inherent in this Element. If you have this appearance, you'll be a dynamo and probably quite driven to accomplish your goals. Many of the most successful men who are Wood are shorter than the general population. The label "short-man syndrome" is often applied to those of lesser stature who have pushed to great success in life. The assumption is that these men are trying to make up for their sense of inferiority due to their height. But in fact, I believe that in most cases, the real factor in their success is their vital Elemental energy pushing through.

If you have the taller type of Wood body, you'll probably express this energy more gently. This body is often paired with a long rectangular face shape—just another sign of that "tree" shape.

Wood: Who Are You? What Is Your Calling?

Who are you, and how can you fall in love with who you really are? How can you clear the way for your true calling to emerge? You must first allow your Wood essence to flourish in order to manifest your purpose in the world. If this is your Element, your true nature contains a primal drive to be active. You're very optimistic and have a bright vitality. Your reason for living is to go out and do, to make your ideas really happen. The strong engine inside you compels you to move forward in a straight line toward your goal. However, Wood also carries the ability for great flexibility, for the tree that can't bend gets blown down in the storm. Channel your dynamic energy toward your goal, yet make sure you're able to yield to others' opinions and needs.

And although you may be adaptable and change with the times, you must still stay true to your Elemental potential and concentrate on defining your place in the world. Find ways to use your greatest strengths: Your confidence, vision, and drive give you a laser focus that can help you achieve any goal. Empower yourself by taking regular time to be active, create the systems that will help you move forward in a decisive way, and never stop growing. When your Wood qi is flowing, life will come into balance and you can encounter new possibilities beyond your wildest dreams.

Chapter 9

FIRE—TO EXCITE

In this chapter, I'll introduce the basics of the Fire Element, and you'll learn how to identify it. To begin, here's a quick-reference list of Fire characteristics:

- **Energy:** peaking, moving upward and outward, activity at its height, noon, summer, prime of life

- **Qualities:** exuberant, joyful, passionate, warm, desires intimacy, loves change, self-centered, fickle, flirtatious, dramatic, physically affectionate, hyperactive, scattered, anxious or prone to panic attacks, short attention span, humorous, fun, overly expressive, inspirational, empathic

- **Major features:** eyes, curly or red hair, tips of features

- **Organ:** heart, small intestines

- **Sense organ:** tongue

What to Look for

You don't need to have *all* of the following aspects for this Element to play a strong role in your life—any of these will indicate that it's a factor in your personality. The more of them you possess, the more Fire there is in your nature:

- Sparkling eyes, "light" in the eyes
- Red and/or curly hair, spiky or extreme hairstyles, balding on top of the head
- Easy smile and laugh
- Quick movements and speech
- Slim hips
- Pink flush to complexion, freckles
- Dimples
- Pointed tips of mouth, nose, ears, eyes, and/or eyebrows

Fig. 59: Fire Face

Fig. 60: Fire Face

How do you know if the Fire Element is a major part of your personality? You look for your strongest features—what's most noticeable in your face. You may not have all or even many of the kinds of features listed above, but if you have red hair or sparkling eyes, you have this Element in your makeup. The more strong features you have from the list, the more of it you have in your personality.

If you're a typical Fire person, you'll have eyes that shine and sparkle. You'll move and talk quickly, with a ready laugh. Your hair may be red or curly, and you might have a pink flush, especially to your cheeks and chest. Your hips will be slim and the tips of some features may be pointed, such as a sharp nose and corners of your eyes, or the ends of your mouth will be tapered. Your energy may

precede you into a room, because you have a glow about you that exudes charisma. If you have all these characteristics, which is rare, you'll know that you're very Fiery!

Well-known faces that show this Element include Billy Crystal, Jack Black, Ashley Judd, and Shirley MacLaine.

The energy of Fire is the thrill of being alive, the passion of living life to the fullest. The force that came into full definition in the Wood stage continues the cycle as Fire, which embodies the desire to consume and be consumed in the pure exuberance of the moment. When something burns, it transforms from the physical into smoke, ash, and vapors rising into the heavens. And the urge of this Element is always toward that feeling of transcending into union with the Divine.

The power of Fire is in the heart—the feeling center and the home of love in the body. Such emotions make the qi in the body rise and disperse, just as a flame flares up. They connect us with our sense of our pure spirit. Affection, joy, passion, and the spiritual illumination that changes your life—all embody the sensation of this Element rising inside you.

In order to transcend your limitations and experience this sense of joyous union, Fire calls you to have an open heart. This is the only way for you to merge entirely with another in a pure experience of love. But this leaves you unprotected, so you must feel safe enough to make yourself accessible to another. Fire people are often highly vulnerable because they can naturally be so unguarded emotionally.

The verb that best describes the quality of this Element is "to excite." As a Fire person, you thrive when you can experience that internal surge of excitement and exuberance on a regular basis throughout the day!

The Personality of Fire

The energy of Fire is illustrated by summer in full force—the exuberance of all nature at its greatest height, flowers in extravagant bloom, and lush leaves, all at their peak life force. It's the strong qi of the young adult, fully developed and feeling a surge of strength and vitality, diving into the experience of life. Fire is noon, when the sun is at its highest point in the sky. This is the excitement of wanting to merge with the world and ultimately with the Divine essence of who we are.

The strength of this personality is exuberance, joy, and the thrill of being alive. If you're Fire, you ride that flare throughout your life, finding fun in everything you do and lighting up the paths of others as you go. You yearn for intimacy, needing to touch and be touched. You're passionate and warm and love change and new experiences since it's the nature of Fire to continue to move to find new things to burn.

The challenge for this Element is overexcitement, which can lead to being scattered, erratic, anxious, or—at its most extreme—hyperactive or prone to panic attacks. When you're stressed, your energy will surge upward too quickly and you can act rashly, which you regret later; this quality also means that you may not be able to stick with anything for very long. And because of Fire's emotional vulnerability, when you're hurt, you can become deeply sad and it will feel difficult to find your way out. You naturally distance yourself from others when you're really upset, but staying home alone only causes you to fall into deeper and deeper despair. To recover, your Fire instead needs to reestablish a connection with others because that's what really nourishes your soul.

The first thing people notice about you when you walk into a room is that you're laughing, joking, and talking a mile a minute! And it can be virtually impossible for you to speak without gesturing with your hands. You may observe people's eyes flitting back and forth from your face to your hands as you talk. Fire is fast—you speak and move quickly, and your mind is so active it never shuts down.

This makes you very adaptable; you love variety and change. For the same reason, you're a great multitasker, but you risk getting overextended and scattered as ideas flood your head or projects stack up on your desk. It can be hard to stay focused—you're just so excited about everything that comes your way! If you do get too scattered, it can create chaos in your life. You'll have difficulty

stopping to organize or gain control of the situation and are more likely to try to find a way to quit altogether and move on to something new.

As a Fire person, you can be frivolous and playful, and you love to flirt with men *and* women . . . and pets, children, and the world at large! You're not necessarily serious; it just feels natural to interact in this way. When it comes to romance, you're crazy about falling in love, but you'd prefer the infatuation stage to last forever. Once things start feeling too settled, you may become dissatisfied and look for new excitement, whether within the relationship or outside of it.

Therefore, Fire can seem a bit fickle socially. You may have many friends, but they may not be deep or lifelong bonds because most people aren't as lively as you are and can't move or think quickly enough for you. When things get difficult, you may want to move on rather than stick around to work on the relationship. Or if you are prone to Fiery moods, you may create drama that can result in some emotional scenes. These unreliable or dramatic sides can be frustrating to your friends of other Elements. They need to find a way to adjust or else move on.

One of my favorite feng-shui clients of many years was a doctor who happened to be a Fire woman. She thought I was very powerful because each time I did some work with her, immediate change occurred in her life. Frankly, that was most likely due more to her quick, changeable Fiery nature than any magic I summoned! Like most others in her Element, she was poised for change and our sessions together let her feel that she had permission to surge ahead.

Her Fire didn't always serve her well, however, as it was frequently out of balance. She had great trouble concentrating and staying organized, forgetting to write notes about her patients and mixing up lab results. And her flirtatious nature lost her at least one opportunity. I had another client, a television producer, who was looking for a doctor to host a new show, and my Fire client friend was perfect—attractive, articulate, and brimming with joy. I arranged for them to get together, but the meeting never happened. The producer went to her home at the agreed-upon time, but there was no answer. She rang, knocked, tried the back door,

and called on her cell phone, waiting 20 minutes before she finally left. It turned out that the doctor was in the basement, flirting with the cute plumber who'd come to make a quick repair, and she'd forgotten all about the TV-show appointment!

It's the nature of Fire to be noticed and seen. If this is your Element, you could end up in the spotlight more often than not, even in small ways. This can be challenging in a friendship: You may rush to the side of your best friend, who's just lost her job and is going through a divorce, but five minutes into the conversation, you're both suddenly talking about *your* new shoes—and it will feel right! It's not that you don't care about others, but no one should go to Fire people for deep commiseration. However, you *do* go to them to feel uplifted, forget about your troubles, and get some fun back into your life.

I've noticed that new mothers who have a lot of this Element tend to have more challenges than many other women. What's one of the main things you must do with a new baby? Stay, stay, and stay. You must always be available, up every few hours for a feeding and always focused on taking care of the baby . . . the same routine, day after day . . . not a very Fiery thing to do. I've seen many clients with this Element who have postpartum depression, highly challenged by a lifestyle that allows so little change and fun.

This isn't to say that Fire people don't make good parents. They absolutely do, but as with all the Elements, they may need some support during times that require a type of energy that's not natural for them. If you're a Fire woman, you especially need help during those early months of motherhood—someone to give you a break and free you to go out to lighten up a bit.

Because Fire supplies such intensity to everything in life, you'll have a tendency to exaggerate. It's not that you intentionally lie— it's just that the facts don't feel powerful enough to communicate the intensity of your actual experience. You won't be able to stop yourself from saying you waited for an hour when it was more like 20 minutes. What you're trying to get across is that you were there for a very long time. You'll declare that the temperature at your vacation resort was 100 degrees every day when it never went past 85—the point is that you were really hot!

If your Fire ever becomes unbalanced, this drama can get out of hand. Your upsets can become huge, wailing performances, or your sadness may spiral out of control so that you're inconsolable. You may make sudden, rash decisions that create havoc in your life and the lives of others.

Years ago, I had a client who worked in a large corporation and was a highly empathic woman, as many Fires are, able to sense when something isn't quite right with a person or place. On the job, she was like a canary in a coal mine: If the subtle energy wasn't in balance, she was the first to notice. When her company had a major reorganization that wasn't going well, she convinced management to fly me in to consult for a few days. During my visit, she picked me up at my hotel and took me to their offices. By the third day, the energy of the people and the space had begun to shift significantly, and my empathic client was feeling it. As we drove in that morning, she described how off center she felt during this transition stage and how it was bringing up all kinds of emotions for her. She became more and more excited and distraught until she was hysterical, shrieking and sobbing at the steering wheel. I managed to convince her to pull over to the curb, where she continued her dramatic wailing while people on the street looked in to see what in the world was going on! Suddenly, a tall, gorgeous woman in a full-length faux-leopard coat swooped by, striding down the street. My client looked up, her face aglow, and said, "But everything would be all right if I could just have that coat!"

Fortunately for you as a Fire person—and for everyone else in your life—if you do get upset, it does tend to pass quickly! The nature of this Element is joy, after all, and you feel much more "yourself" being happy than upset.

Fire Style

— **Clothing:** This Element has fun with clothes. As a Fire woman, you can pull off quirky, dramatic combinations that might look ridiculous on anyone else—plaid, fur, and lace . . . with cowboy boots—and you look fabulous. You'd sleep in high heels if you

could and love stilettos with pointed toes. You prefer sexy fashions, often in vivid colors or animal prints; and will always want to wear things that are pretty, fun, and make you feel delectable. This can seem like flamboyance or vanity to others, but it's your nature to want to express your natural exuberance with your clothes, just as you do with every other aspect of your life.

— **Home:** You'll probably prefer dramatic, fun, or unusual architecture and décor. You love avant-garde furniture, playful accent pieces, extreme or eccentric artwork, and strong colors. You may have collections of toys on display, candles burning everywhere, or walls painted saturated hues of crimson, orange, or violet. Anything new and on the cutting edge of design fits your personality.

Your house will function best if you can use any room for a variety of purposes. If you work at home, I advise having at least three desks or work spaces, as it will allow you to be Fiery in your approach to projects. This Element likes to spend 10 minutes on one thing, change to another for 20 minutes, then switch to a new one, and so on. One challenge can be clutter, as you'll have so many projects going at the same time that there will probably be stacks of things left half done. Fire's short attention span can be a real problem in keeping it all organized.

— **Movement:** Because Fire loves to have fun and doesn't focus on anything for long, you'll avoid any exercise that's repetitive, boring, or takes a long time to do. Any activity that allows fast movement and change, on the other hand, will appeal to you. An exercise program that includes a lot of variety will be the only thing that works for you. You'll also enjoy moving to music and will especially love dancing if it involves a partner you can flirt with!

— **Profession:** You're great with other people and extremely talented at communicating, so you could easily end up in a related career. You're superb in public relations and marketing and can excel at sales because your warm, upbeat personality makes your clients feel better the minute you walk in the door. This Element is a natural at performing, so you'll find a lot of actors in this category,

as well as teachers and public speakers. A well-balanced Fire has a wonderful ability to take people to great heights, inspiring them to recognize and use the best in themselves.

Perhaps you've recognized yourself or a friend in the descriptions above, and it may have given you new insights and awareness. But you may feel that while you see *some* Fire, it doesn't completely describe you or your friend. Remember that while we all have some of each of the five Elements in our personalities, usually one or two are emphasized—some people even have four of the Elements strongly in their faces and are weak in only one. So it may be as you read this book that you can identify a second, third, or even fourth category that gives you a complete understanding of who you are inside.

But even if you don't find Fire features emphasized in your face, you still have eyes, tips of features, and so on! In the next chapter, we'll examine each of these features individually and learn what they can tell us in more detail about how Fire manifests in your inherent spirit.

Chapter 10

READING THE FIRE FEATURES

As I've mentioned, in addition to giving the entire face a certain look, each Element corresponds with specific facial features. In this chapter, you'll learn how to gain even more insight into the Fire Element from each of these body parts.

Eyes

Aside from observing the smiles and laughter in your bright face, the most important indication of Fire in your personality is the light in your eyes. You'll see sparkling brightness and clarity—a gleam shining through. It will be easy to detect this in some people, but overall, the ability to see it is a skill you'll develop after a bit of practice.

While your eyes show us if you have this Element, they have many other secrets to share. One secret they reveal is how you feel about communicating with others, and their size is meaningful in this regard. Although their natural size is significant, even more important is how wide open you hold them. If you have naturally large eyes but keep them narrowed, or if you were born with small eyes but hold them wide open, this is valuable information about your attitude with respect to exchanging thoughts and feelings.

Eyes that are large or that are held wide open (Fig. 61) are usually a sign that it's natural for you to express your feelings. It probably wouldn't even occur to you to hide what you're thinking in any situation. This can make for great friendships because you're openly affectionate and people never have to wonder what's going on or if you have a private agenda. However, you may wear your heart on your sleeve, which can cause difficulties for you. You might fall in love too quickly or trust too easily, creating the possibility that someone might take advantage of you or hurt your feelings.

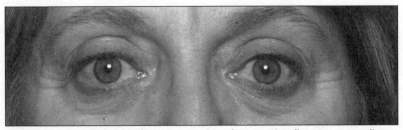

Fig. 61: Eyes that are held wide open are a sign of an emotionally open personality.

Eyes that appear extremely large can be a symptom of a physical imbalance, especially if they seem to be bulging out. But in cases where this isn't due to illness, they can also be an indication of a "drama queen"—someone who's highly emotional and unable to keep anything inside.

Alternatively, this type of feature can indicate that you're a highly sensitive person who takes in too much "communication" from the people and places around you. Eyes like these are a sign that you've had to learn to be constantly vigilant, scanning your environment for anything that could throw you off balance. Perhaps you were emotionally traumatized to some degree as a child or, due to your open nature, just experiencing the intense emotions expressed in your family sent your system into overload early on. The result is that you make your eyes even bigger than before, trying to perceive any danger before it can reach you.

If someone's eyes open very wide as they speak to you, it's a sign that they're excited about what they're saying. But if they do this on a consistent basis, it can reveal that they may be feeling an all-consuming desire to reach out and connect with others. When this happens to the extreme, the individual might even go to the point of obsession with another person.

If you hold your eyes in a more narrowed fashion (Fig. 62), there's a limit to just how much communication you're willing to accept from others without evaluation. In any relationship, whether personal or professional, you won't be gullible. You're more skeptical and probably think of yourself as a realist. You may find it hard to trust people and can be suspicious of their motives. You're excellent, however, at thinking things out logically and have acute perceptive abilities. If someone wants to convince you of anything, they'll have to work hard for that honor.

If you have narrowed eyes, you'll tend to guard how much you're willing to share your inner self, even in intimate relationships. You won't express your emotions easily and may consider it shallow and silly to do so. You actually feel things very deeply but could have difficulty letting these emotions out when the time is right. You'll take longer to fall in love, but when you do, you'll give yourself deeply and completely.

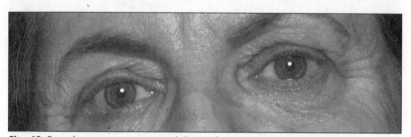

Fig. 62: Eyes that are more narrowed show a less emotionally open nature.

The Set of the Eyes

Sometimes, however, it's not about how you hold your eyes, but how deeply or shallowly set they naturally are in your face. If you're not sure about your eye set, there's a test to find out. Take your index finger and hold it vertically in front of your eye. Bring

your finger closer to your eye until you place the top of your finger against your eyebrow, and lay the bottom part of your finger against your upper cheek. (You can close your eye.) As you hold your finger there, if you can't feel your eyeball, then your eyes are deep set. If you *can* feel it, they're "shallow set." This gives you information about how you'll communicate.

Shallow-set eyes are similar to the wide-held ones described above: You'll more naturally be forthcoming about what's going on inside, and you'll also be more open to input from others. This can be a wonderful quality, but if you're too easily influenced by what others are saying or doing, it can be a challenge as well.

If your eyes are deep set (Fig. 63), you'll be much more reserved than most people. Even more than those with narrowed eyes, you won't easily share your thoughts and feelings with others; you'll evaluate a situation privately instead of jumping in to offer your opinion. One of my students with these eyes said with a mischievous smile, "Yes, I'll let you talk and talk—but you may never know what *I* think!"

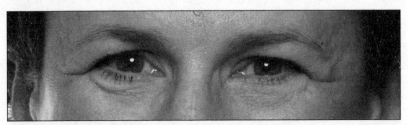

Fig. 63: Deep-set eyes indicate a more private temperament.

If you have narrowed, deep-set eyes, you probably have a very hard time communicating feelings or being open with others. You may have hidden emotions that you don't feel capable of sharing easily or believe that others will simply never understand you. This can sometimes translate as a person who will naturally carry suspicion toward everyone they meet or who will have difficulty trusting anyone.

Eye Slant

Eye slant also reveals important information. You determine the angle of this feature by measuring whether the outer corners are higher than the inner ones. Draw an imaginary line from the inside point of your eye straight across to the outer one. In most people, they're at the same level. But if the outer corner is higher (Fig. 64), it's a sign of overall optimism and cleverness. You're also likely to be ambitious and even opportunistic because your quick mind can see more possibilities in any situation.

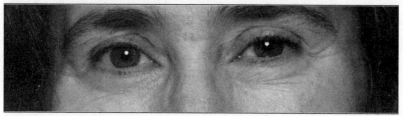

Fig. 64: Upturned eyes reveal a clever, positive personality.

If the outer corner of your eye appears lower than the inner corner (Fig. 65), this is a sign of a very kind nature. If you fit this description, you almost risk being taken advantage of because of your soft heart. These eyes also show a tendency toward pessimism or a sense of sadness that can make you give up too easily.

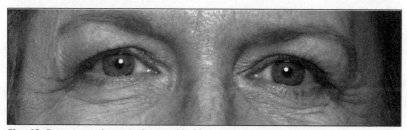

Fig. 65: Downturned eyes indicate a kind but more pessimistic nature.

There are a few other things to be learned specifically by looking at your eyelids, which are excellent indicators of your perception of others and how you'll behave in any situation.

The lower eyelid is a mirror of your approach and response to others. If it's curved (Fig. 66), you'll care very much about people's experiences with you—again, any roundness on a feature is added warmth and tact. You'll want everyone involved with you to come away with a positive result, and you'll aim for kindness in all communications.

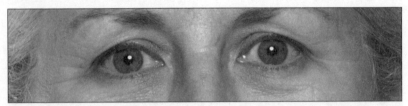

Fig. 66: A curved lower eyelid shows some additional openness and warmth.

If your lower eyelid instead goes across in a straight line (Fig. 67), you're more likely to survey a situation with an emphasis on logic or common sense over emotions. In negotiations, you won't lose sight of the need to focus on what will best help you achieve your goal, and you'll always keep the bottom line in mind. If you're involved in a project with someone with lower eyelids that are straight, you'll need to be aware that they won't be too concerned about how the outcome affects you.

Fig. 67: A straight lower eyelid shows an emphasis on logic over emotions.

If your upper eyelid comes down to cover some of the iris (Fig. 68), you'll tend to be fair and objective and will always look at others' points of view. You may, however, be a bit secretive about your own feelings. You might size someone up for quite a while before deciding whether to share what you truly think. If your eyelid goes this low, you're very private, and most people may never know the real truth inside you.

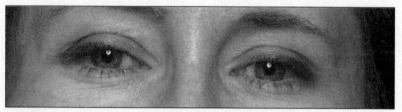

Fig. 68: The upper eyelid covering part of the iris indicates a private person.

Joy Lines

Many people have what are usually called "crow's-feet" at the sides of their eyes (Fig. 69). These are called "joy lines" in Chinese face reading, and they come as a result of that wonderful Fire emotion, causing marks from smiles and laughter. These are definitely wrinkles that we all want to develop.

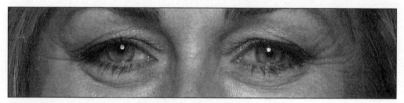

Fig. 69: Wrinkles by the sides of the eyes are joy lines.

Overall, people with this Element will wrinkle more and sooner than most of the others. Your quick nature can run through so many emotions in a very short period of time! And because Fire is about communication, these feelings will create more expressions, which in turn cause wrinkles. However, the good news is that most of the marks will be associated with excitement and joy. They'll show up as lines around your eyes and mouth as a result of smiling, laughing, and making exaggerated faces as you communicate your exuberance.

White-Sided Eyes

When you look directly into your eyes in the mirror, you see the sclera—the whites on either side of the iris. But in some cases, you might also see the whites below the iris, above it, or both. In general, these are cases of imbalance in this Element due to an overactive nervous system. You've been using up your Fire qi and have become highly stressed as a result. In this situation, you can be reactive, hypersensitive, touchy, or even irrational. This is often a temporary condition, usually due to tension, exhaustion, or illness. If you see this in your face, it's a sign that you need to make time to rest and rejuvenate in order to come back into balance.

In Japan, this appearance is called *"sanpaku"* and is considered to be a sign that someone is in danger of dying; traditional Chinese face reading also subscribes to this belief. If this was true, however, many of my clients would have passed on by now! The truth is that white-sided eyes do indeed show that you're highly stressed and may be accident-prone or vulnerable to illness because of it, which might explain the association with the possibility of death. And in the long run, if you keep living off your Fire in this way, it can burn up all your "jing"—the reserves of energy I discussed in the chapter on the Water Element—and shorten your life.

If the lower whites of your eyes are visible (Fig. 70), this shows a current Fire imbalance, which can be the result of pressure and overwork. It could also mean an overactive or hyperactive nervous system, resulting in high anxiety or even panic attacks. If this is the case, you're becoming tightly wound and may be so stressed that you're taking everything personally. At its extreme, this is an indicator that you could even be on the edge of violence.

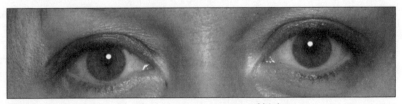

Fig. 70: Whites visible under the irises are a symptom of high stress.

When the upper whites of your eyes are visible (Fig. 71), it shows an ongoing Fire imbalance with the same potential as the previous issue, but less of an immediate danger. This is more of a chronic condition, indicating continual feelings of high anxiety. You can be overly sensitive in any relationship and take every-thing personally. It does also include the possibility of becoming extremely nervous and even hysterical, or over the long term it can point to the development of a more serious emotional disorder.

Fig. 71: Whites visible above the irises show chronic stress.

After September 11, 2001, when photographs of the terrorists were published in the newspaper, I was astonished to see how this effect was demonstrated. A large percentage of them had white vis-ible on three sides of their eyes. These pictures weren't taken just before they'd boarded the planes that day. Rather, these were visa and passport images that were made long before that tragic day, but they showed high levels of stress and probably their willingness—if not intentions—to die. It was chilling.

If both the upper and lower whites are visible—in other words if you can see the whites all around someone's eyes—it's a sign of either madness or genius. This is Fire full blast and can't be main-tained for long without burnout.

A few years ago, there was a lot of publicity about Jennifer Wilbanks, the "Runaway Bride" who'd been under such stress that she disappeared right before her wedding, causing great anguish for her friends and family and inconvenience for local authorities. The public didn't get a look at her face until after she'd returned home, but the moment I saw her eyes, I recognized just how much stress she'd been under. The whites were highly visible all around

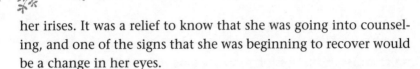
her irises. It was a relief to know that she was going into counseling, and one of the signs that she was beginning to recover would be a change in her eyes.

For public figures, signs of sanpaku *are* held to mean the possibility of impending assassination or fatal accident. There are official photos of Abraham Lincoln and John F. Kennedy that show this clearly. Reportedly, Robert Kennedy; Martin Luther King, Jr.; John Lennon; Princess Diana; and John F. Kennedy, Jr., showed white-sided eyes before they died, although I haven't seen documentation in these cases.

Aside from the logic that a leader under tremendous and pervasive pressure could become accident-prone, there's a theory about why he might be at specific risk for assassination. Because of the incredible demands and responsibilities he copes with, his system becomes stressed and weakened. When he's compromised in this way, the public unconsciously reads this in his face, just as animals read such signs in the wild. In nature, when the head of a pack becomes weak, he's said to develop the same indications in his eyes, and he may then be attacked and killed by another member. Although this sounds terrible, it actually assures the preservation of the group because they need a strong and healthy leader in order to survive. So a person who's mentally imbalanced with a potential for violence, someone who's acting out of his "animal brain" without impulse control, may instinctively react to the sight of white-sided eyes in a public figure and strike out at him.

However, for someone living a normal life, this feature will only mean that you need to rebalance your health and lifestyle! At the end of a lecture I gave in New York once, an elderly Chinese woman came up to me with tears streaming down her face. She said that a decade earlier, she'd gone to a face reader in Chinatown who told her that she had the same eyes as John F. Kennedy, which meant that she was about to die. She'd been in constant dread ever since that moment, waiting to pass away. She sobbed as she told me that the way I described this condition had explained everything, and she felt released from the terrible fear she'd carried for so many years. Can you imagine?!

Types of Hair

If you have red hair, or even brown hair with warm highlights, you have Fire. Curly hair also means this Element is present in your personality—and by this I mean very curly; if your hair is wavy, this is Water instead. And yes, coloring or curling your hair will add more Fire to your nature, as can choosing a spiky or extreme hairstyle. Additionally, baldness or thinning also indicates this Element, almost as if the hair had been burned off by inner heat! Shaving your head adds Fire to your nature as well.

Tips of Features

Fire sears as it moves, scorching the edges of things. If you have this Element, the tips of one or more features may be pointed or peaked. This will have an additional effect of Fire acting on another Element—meaning, for example, that excitability will be added to whatever other emotion that body part controls.

— **Pointed ears:** They aren't common, but if you have these, they show a tendency toward extreme or volatile emotions. Because the ears are associated with the Water Element, the strengthened emotion would be fear. The added Fire could mean that you'll feel the influence of Fiery overexcitement when you're frightened. For instance, you could overreact in some way, becoming highly upset or making an unwise decision based on apprehension or hurt feelings.

— **Pointed mouth corners:** This feature (Fig. 72) indicates that you have a bit of extra Fire in your personality that may appear in your relationships more than anywhere else. And whether your mouth is pointed or not, if the corners curve upward when your mouth is at rest, it signifies a naturally positive outlook, a quality we should all cultivate.

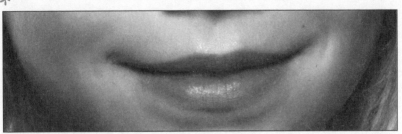

Fig. 72: A mouth with pointed corners is a sign of Fire.

— **Cleft chin:** Although we talked about this feature in a chapter on the Water Element, a chin with a cleft or dimple in it is actually a sign of Fire because the sign is located on the tip of the chin (Fig. 73). This is usually called the mark of a performer. You have a strong need to be acknowledged and appreciated, which can manifest in a few different ways: You could easily be the person everyone likes to have around because you're so much fun and can even be called "the life of the party." You might, however, be extroverted and demanding of attention. You may also be a "pleaser," wanting everyone to like you—or you may simply have a strong desire for your efforts to be noticed. Never assume that this characteristic is the sign of a vain desire for attention. This is a genuine need in your life, and if it isn't filled, you won't be happy.

It's interesting to see how many people in the public eye have cleft chins! As you watch TV and films, you may become aware of the high percentage of actors who fit this description. And even on the evening news when they stop to interview the "man on the street," they always seem to end up with a guy who has this characteristic. Again, we see how our energy will naturally manifest in the world without us having to do anything.

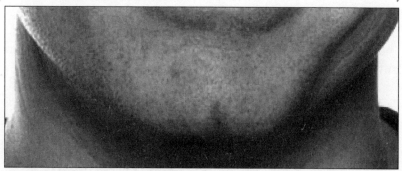

Fig. 73: A cleft chin is said to indicate the personality of a performer.

— **Sharp inner corners of the eyes:** This is also a sign of additional Fire. Because the eyes are especially associated with communication style and ability, they reveal how you speak to others. If the inner canthus (inner corners) are pointed (Fig. 74), it means that you can be very precise in your exchanges with others. You can also be described as having a "sharp tongue," because when you're agitated, you'll tend to lash out with words or have trouble censoring how you feel.

If the inner canthus of your eye not only points but curves downward like a claw (Fig. 75), this is a more extreme version of the sharp tongue. If you're ever deeply upset, you have the potential to attack with words, intentionally saying hurtful things to strike back at those who have injured you.

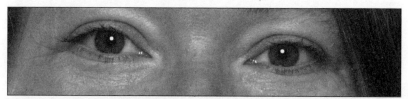

Fig. 74: A pointed inner canthus shows a "sharp tongue."

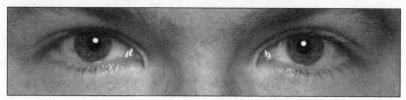

Fig. 75: A hooked inner canthus shows the potential to be vicious in communications.

— **Pointed tip of nose:** A pointed tip of the nose (Fig. 76) represents your tendency to be curious—you love to "find out why," and you'll be interested in pursuing things in detail. It can also be an indication that you're less likely to be naturally trusting of others.

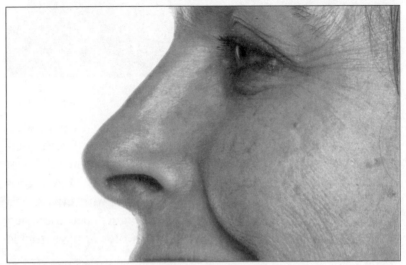

Fig. 76: A pointed tip of the nose indicates a curious nature.

A full or rounded tip of the nose (Fig. 77) is a sign that you especially like the creature comforts in life. You may enjoy cooking, collecting, or the pleasure of creating a welcoming home.

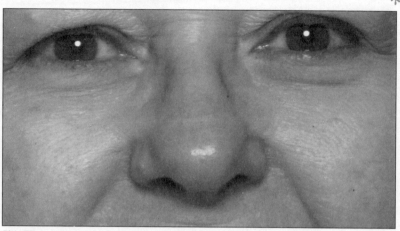

Fig. 77: A rounded nose tip reflects enjoyment of the pleasures of life.

The tip of the nose is also where you gauge your level of emotional vulnerability. In Chinese medicine, there's a part of the heart called the "heart protector" that's associated with the pericardium, the membrane surrounding the organ. Sometimes called the guardian to the "gate of intimacy," its energetic function is to protect the emotional center from being hurt. A healthy defender will open the gate to beneficial experiences—anything that will contribute to your health and growth—but screen out harmful ones. If it's been weakened, there's more risk of being too vulnerable.

If you see a vertical line at the very tip of your nose (Fig. 78), it indicates that you might be too openhearted and have been (or can be) more easily hurt in relationships. If this mark appears within a short period of time, it could represent the fact that you've become too exposed emotionally or your heart has been broken recently.

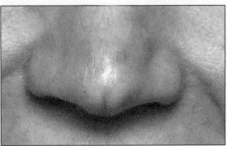

Fig. 78: A cleft in the tip of the nose can mean emotional vulnerability.

Remember that a feature can also be a meaningful indicator of the state of your physical health. Some doctors of Chinese medicine state that the tip of the nose is where you can see the health of the heart. Any sudden changes here—in shape, coloration, or markings—may be signs of a physical imbalance developing.

Dimples

Lastly, dimples in the cheeks (Fig. 79) are another sign of Fire and mean that you have an extra dose of charm and magnetism!

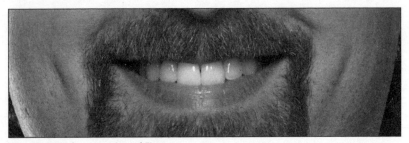

Fig. 79: Dimples are a sign of Fire.

Fire: Who Are You? What Is Your Calling?

Who are you, and how can you fall in love with who you really are? How can you clear the way for your true calling to emerge?

You must first allow your Fire essence to flourish in order to manifest your purpose in the world. If this is your Element, your true nature is one that carries within it a pure exuberance and the thrill of being alive. Your lifelong desire is to merge with others in this joyous warmth; intimacy and heart-to-heart connections are why you live and breathe. Don't deny yourself opportunities for this nourishment.

Find ways to use your greatest strengths: your bright spirit, desire for intimate connection, and true inspirational ability. Don't suppress this energy when it arises. Instead, allow and acknowledge your vulnerability while having the discernment that will protect your heart from being hurt. Give yourself a life where you can have variety, change, and plenty of whatever makes that rush of exuberance soar through your body. When your Fire qi is flowing, life will come into balance, and you can encounter new possibilities beyond your wildest dreams.

Chapter 11

EARTH—TO NURTURE

In this chapter, I'll introduce the basics of the Earth Element, and you'll learn how to identify it. To begin, here's a quick-reference list of Earth characteristics:

- **Energy:** downward moving, settling, afternoon, late summer/early fall, middle age

- **Qualities:** giving, caring, helpful, diplomatic, sympathetic, worried, indecisive, patient, friendly, thoughtful, tolerant, grounded, stuck/stagnant, needy, self-pitying, overprotective, overinvolved in others' lives, supportive, kind, modest, dependent, focused on family and friends

- **Major features:** mouth, lower cheeks, bridge of nose, area above upper lip, upper eyelid

- **Organs:** stomach, spleen, pancreas

- **Sense organ:** mouth

What to Look for

You don't need to have *all* of the following aspects for this Element to play a strong role in your life—any of these will indicate that it's a factor in your personality. The more of them you possess, the more Earth there is in your nature:

- Round face
- Roundness to the body, especially the stomach
- Generous mouth in comparison to rest of features
- Full lips
- Full and/or softly rounded lower cheeks
- Large breasts in women; large muscles in men
- Thick calves
- Yellow-hued complexion

Fig. 80: Earth Face

Fig. 81: Earth Face

How do you know if the Earth Element is a major part of your personality? You look for your strongest features—what "speaks" to you most in your face. You may not have all or even many of the kinds of features listed above, but if you have a round face or full lips, you have this Element in your makeup. The more strong Earth features you have, the more of this energy you have in your personality.

Well-known faces that show this Element include Renée Zellweger, Hillary Clinton, Oprah Winfrey, Rosie O'Donnell, and Dolly Parton (Earth and Fire together!).

If you're a typical Earth, you may have full cheeks and a tendency toward a round stomach, no matter what your weight. You could have large muscles and thick limbs, especially your lower

legs. Compared to the rest of the features on your face, your mouth may be large and/or your lips full. There may be a slight yellowish tinge to your complexion, but this can be difficult for a novice to detect. If you have all of these characteristics, which is rare, you'll know that you're a very Earthy person!

The Personality of Earth

This energy has to do with harvest time. The fruit is ripe, falling off the trees, and it's time for feasting and nourishing the body. It's a stable period of little work or struggle; and it's about community, with family and friends coming together to eat and enjoy. Earth is the afternoon, when you feel heavy from lunch and sit at your desk, not wanting to work very hard. It's middle age, when you've accomplished much of what you were aiming for and now don't feel as driven; it's about pausing to rest, ingest nourishment, and absorb the benefits of your hard work.

This Element is associated with the archetype of the Mother, whose great strength is her tremendously caring, giving nature. These people are the best friends in the world because they truly care about you and want to be there for you in every way. If you're Earth, your first thought is *How can I help?* Your sympathetic, affectionate nature makes you reach out in friendship to whoever comes into your life.

The power of this Element is in the home, family, comfort, and security. It calls us to remember the importance of connection, grounding, and the receptiveness that allows us to give and receive the embrace of love in our lives.

You can easily be recognized as Earth if you want to feed people as soon as they come to your home—and if they won't eat, you may start to twitch. This Element is about nurturing and taking care of others; you have an inherent need to give and to help people. As such, relationships are very important to you, and family and friends are a big part of your life. You'll be the one who maintains photo albums or makes scrapbooks commemorating everyone's special moments.

At the end of a lecture I gave in the Midwest, I asked for a volunteer from the audience for a face-reading demonstration. A sea of hands shot up, and I chose someone who could easily come to the front of the room, who turned out to be a very sweet Earth woman. As I talked about what I was observing in her face, I could see out of the corner of my eye that she was gradually becoming more and more uncomfortable. It's common in these situations for someone to suddenly become very self-conscious when she realizes that she's volunteered to stand in front of a crowd of strangers and let them stare at her! But I did a quick mental review to find out if I'd said anything tactless that might have hurt her feelings and could only conclude that I was embarrassing her with all the nice things I was saying about her.

By then she was visibly squirming and finally reached into her purse. Puzzled, I turned toward her, and she began to hand me pieces of candy. In alignment with her true nature, this Earth woman was trying to feed me!

This urge to nurture extends to the business world as well. As Earth, you're thoughtful and careful with your work, and you tend to be modest about your talents. But you're the one who can make the difference in the success or failure of any venture. I once did a private consultation for one of the wealthiest entrepreneurs in Europe, a man who was purely Wood Element and who had a history of coming up with brilliant ideas. He'd launch a new project and quickly earn millions of euros. But then a year or two later, he'd be on to his next idea and the previous venture would collapse behind him. His Wood energy made him not want to stick around and have to tend to management and long-term planning. I helped him use face reading to hire an Earth person to run his newest business for him so that it would be well cared for and continue to thrive.

Faithful, sympathetic, and sentimental in relationships, you need people in your life who are emotionally open and available because a full connection is the only one that will satisfy you. You'd rather be with others than alone; and when you're by yourself, you're probably planning the next time you'll see a friend. This is like the proverbial Mother thinking about what to cook for dinner as she's washing the breakfast dishes.

But every Element has its challenges, and yours is your tendency to worry. It's the energy of the caretaker to have her mind busy with how she's going to fill the needs of those who depend on her. But you may feel so distressed by thoughts and worries that it's difficult to think clearly. In the body, Earth is associated with the stomach and digestion. There's an aspect of worry that has to do with thoughts not being well "digested" in the mind. Rather than processing thoughts and moving on, you can tend to go over and over them, like a cow chewing her cud!

This Element can be needy or even become resentful over time, which is the negative archetype of Mother: overinvolved, obsessing about details, nagging, or intrusive. Because you care so much about the people you love, you can become too caught up in their lives, just like a mom fretting about her children. This can be very frustrating for everyone and creates opportunities for misunderstanding and hurt feelings. It's likely that if a relationship ends, it's not your choice, and you may have a hard time letting go.

One of my Earth clients permanently lost a friend because of her eagerness for connection. She had been thrilled to develop a bond with a woman in her community who shared her hobbies. They began to spend a lot of time together, but it never felt like enough for the Earth woman. She began to drop in on her new acquaintance at all hours, even without an invitation, unable to control her impulse to deepen their attachment. When her friend became ill with a cold, my client was at her door with homemade soup, eager to nurture her—but she was the type of person who wanted to be alone when she was sick, so she refused to answer the door! This upset my client so much that she deluged her with phone calls to see how she was feeling and when they could arrange a visit. This was the last straw for her new friend, who declared that the relationship was over. The Earth woman was consumed with guilt and obsessed for months about how she could possibly rejuvenate things.

Moving Past Challenges

When you think of Earth, visualize the solid ground or a mountain, an unmoving stability. So as a member of this Element, change isn't your favorite thing; instead, you enjoy predictability. In your career, you'll be the most uncomfortable with reorganization or a move. You may enjoy travel, but your best memories will revolve around the new friendships you made and the meals you had, and you'll be sure to buy lots of mementos to put on display in your home to remind you of your trip. Because of your tendency to avoid change, one problem is that you can get stuck in life more easily than any other Element. It's the nature of Earth to be unmoving, and once you settle in, it can be hard to get going again. This can apply to staying in a job beyond the time you've stopped enjoying it, remaining in a relationship too long, or not dealing with life issues that you need to change.

Because you love to be surrounded by your favorite things (and there are probably many of them!), you can have a problem with clutter. This is especially true if you're one of the many Earth people who loves to go to garage sales or antique shops. However, even in this age of clutter-clearing fads, it's not a good idea for your friends to tow a Dumpster up to your home and clear everything out! You'd go into withdrawal. You need your stuff more than any other Element, so a much gentler hand is necessary in your case. It's also advisable to make sure there's plenty of storage in your home because you'll need some level of accumulation to feel comfortable.

I was once asked to come in as a feng-shui consultant to give a second opinion. This very Earthy woman, a best-selling author, had her house feng-shuied by someone a friend had recommended, but she was so upset by what she'd been told she needed to do that she felt she should get the information double-checked, just in case there had been a mistake. When I entered her living room, she nervously told me that this was the room that the consultant had declared was a terrible problem.

I looked around and saw her big easy chair and footstool facing a beautiful massive fireplace, its mantel an altar to her relationships, with photos of family, friends, and the places she'd visited.

The walls were lined with shelves filled with her personal library of books.

I asked her what she used the room for. "This is my sanctuary!" she exclaimed, her voice full of emotion. "I come here when I need to be inspired. All these books are by my favorite authors, and when I sit here, I feel as though I just soak in all their wisdom."

The previous consultant, however, had declared the space disorganized, and said that she should get rid of two-thirds of the shelves' contents. This felt like extreme surgery to my client—and to me, as well! While the books gave a very Earthy sense of fullness and abundance, they weren't crammed together or stacked on top of each other. In fact, you could feel the loving care put into their arrangement. I placed a silent bet that the original feng-shui consultant was a judgmental Wood type for whom this room would indeed be too crowded! I told the woman that she shouldn't change a thing.

It's important to note, however, that a buildup of possessions can still be a serious problem for the Earth person. It can be caused by stagnation in your life, and it contributes to that "stuckness" increasing. It can be a sign that you're feeling overly worried or less clearheaded, and it may also signal depression.

Earth can also have "cluttered" thoughts, which can lead to inefficient work—that is, not being able to be concise and efficient, like the grocery-store cashier who gets so caught up in conversation with a customer that she's not aware of the long line behind him. In general, confusion or indecision can be a major problem for you. You can worry so much that your mind becomes muddled.

Last, guilt may also be a factor in making it difficult to see a situation clearly. As you saw in the story of the broken friendship I told earlier, the energy of this Element means that you'll probably be overly concerned with the feelings of others or feel bad about how you've handled something within a relationship. The mind can become so full of chatter that there's no space left for clarity to emerge, which makes coming to a conclusion very difficult. In any case, you often prefer to not have to make many decisions because they usually mean change—the thing that Earth likes the least!

Earth Style

— **Clothing:** Comfort is a top priority, and you'll always choose that over style. For this reason, loose-fitting clothing is a favorite. You'll also avoid tight waistbands in clothes because this Element tends to give you more of a tummy. Your colors are warm Earth tones such as yellow, gold, pink, and beige. You'll love to wear a sweater that was a gift from a friend or a T-shirt that holds good memories for you. You'll be happiest at home in your soft chenille bathrobe and fuzzy slippers or comfy sweats. You'll probably prefer flatter shoes with rounded toes and will avoid pointy heels at all costs.

— **Home:** Because your favorite position is sitting, we'll find at least one big overstuffed chair or couch in your home, with everything in easy reach—books, remote control, cup of tea, and plate of cookies (or beer and chips!)—so that you can sit still as long as possible and not have to get up. You won't mind smaller rooms since they feel homey and warm. Earth abodes tend to be cozy, often with country décor or plenty of items on display, such as personal mementos, collections, and especially family pictures. It's not uncommon for an entire wall or table to be covered with photos of every friend and relative. Seasonal decorations on the front door and porch are favorites—anything that creates the sense of the family home. You may even have a special room for crafts and love to create handmade gifts for the people in your life.

It may be very helpful to find areas where you can group together some of your special possessions, instead of having them spread all over the house. This can help you continue to feel well nourished by your belongings but still create some clear and open space as well.

— **Movement:** Well, if you're purely Earth, you'd be perfectly content not having to exercise at all! Without that option, anything that can be done with one or more other people works well. You probably won't stay with a regimen that requires a lot of exertion or requires you to wear skimpy clothing, and having to learn how to use specialized equipment isn't at all supportive of Earth energy.

An exercise class you can attend with friends is great, and walking with a companion is a wonderful way to fulfill your need for connection while still getting a healthy workout.

— **Profession:** You're a good collaborator and excel in partnerships, and you're much happier working this way than alone. Skilled at supporting projects or individuals, you're thoughtful and good with details; you can sit still to finish what others have started. Wood should seek you out to help with all the new ideas they've just initiated!

Because relationships are so important in your life, and due to your tolerant and diplomatic nature, you'll find success in any career involving others. Teaching, customer relations, sales, management, administration, teamwork, and diplomacy are all things you do brilliantly. People naturally trust you more than any other Element, as they unconsciously read your features and know that they'll be safe and taken care of. Politicians do well if they have some Earth in their faces.

Perhaps you've recognized yourself or a friend in the descriptions above, and it may have given you new insights and awareness. But you may feel that while you see some Earth, it doesn't completely describe you or your friend. Remember that while we all have some of each of the five Elements in our personalities, usually one or two are emphasized—some people even have four of the Elements strongly in their faces and are weak in only one. So it may be as you read this book, you can identify a second, third, or even fourth category that gives you a complete understanding.

But even if you don't find Earth features emphasized in your face, you still have a mouth, cheeks, and so on! In the next chapter, we'll examine each of these features individually and learn what they can tell us in more detail about how Earth manifests in your inherent spirit.

Chapter 12

READING THE EARTH FEATURES

As I've mentioned, in addition to giving the entire face a certain look, each Element corresponds with specific facial features. In this chapter, you'll learn how to gain even more insight into the Earth Element from each of these body parts.

Mouth

The mouth is the feature most representative of how much Earth energy you have, but it's also a very significant part of the face to read, whether you have that Element or not, because it "speaks" about so many things. Your mouth tells how emotionally available you are in relationships, how generous you can be, and your feelings about "home" and safety in your life. It can reflect your experience with your mother or whoever your caregiver was as a child and about how you are as a nurturer yourself. It's the major indicator of the health of your digestive system as well.

As always, you determine the size of your mouth in relation to the rest of the features on your face; what's big on one person might be small on another. But there's a specific way that you can measure: Draw two imaginary vertical lines down from the center of the irises of your eyes. If these lines intersect with the ends of your mouth, it's a normal size for your face. If it extends past these lines, it's large; if it doesn't touch these boundaries, it's small.

A large mouth (Fig. 82) indicates that you're a generous person overall. Relationships are important to you, as is establishing a good "home base" in some way, whether it's in your personal life, career, or both.

Fig. 82: A large mouth reflects the importance of relationships.

A small mouth (Fig. 83) can mean the opposite. You may be less able or interested in having many relationships, unless there are other features on the face that diminish this effect. It can also reflect a sense of feeling less safe overall. I often find that people with *very* small mouths tend not to establish a permanent home or long-term relationship; they may move often or never have the need to buy, or settle in to, any specific place with a particular person. Or they report lifelong dissatisfaction or frustration, never finding a locale or a relationship that really feels like home to them.

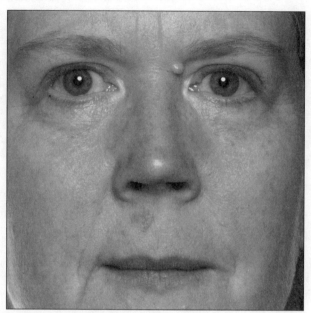

Fig. 83: A small mouth can indicate less of a need for many relationships.

The lips give further information: If both your upper and lower lips are full, you're a sensual, emotionally expressive person. The stereotype of full lips, especially on a woman, is that the person is highly sexual, but that actually isn't the case with either gender. They mean that you have many ways to enjoy having a physical body, sex being only one of them. In fact, this feature is a sign that you may be *less* focused on sex as your main source of pleasure, since you can easily find so many things to relish in life.

If you have an upper lip that is significantly thicker than your lower (Fig. 84), it still indicates generosity and an emotional nature, but the added quality is one of desiring intense emotional experiences. If there isn't enough drama in your life, you'll create it!

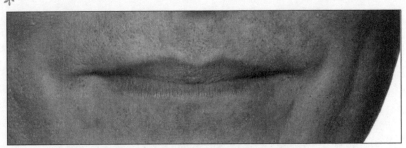

Fig. 84: A thicker upper lip shows the desire for intense experiences.

If you have a thicker lower lip (Fig. 85), you'll long for comfort and love to be pampered. You may also be prone to overindulge, whether in food, sex, or another of life's pleasures.

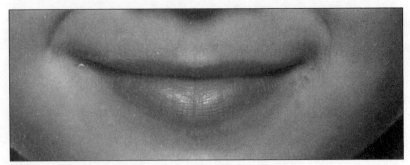

Fig. 85: A thicker lower lip shows a potential for overindulgence.

A flaccid or loose-looking lower lip can indicate poor self-control. This can show up in any number of ways—for example, talking too much, speaking without thinking, or lacking overall discipline, even to the point of hedonistic behavior. But it's important to remember that a feature can reflect an emotional or physical issue, or both. This type of feature could instead reveal the existence of digestive problems in the lower intestine, not poor self-control emotionally; or it could indicate that a person has *both* of these challenges.

Thin lips in a wide mouth show that you may be generous with material things, but perhaps not as available emotionally; thick lips in a wide mouth are a sign that you're very generous in many ways.

A small mouth with full lips is also called a Cupid's Bow (Fig. 86). If you have this kind of mouth, you may sometimes be called self-indulgent. You may never use your potential to manipulate others by pouting if you don't get what you want, but you could use it to great advantage if you chose to. Overall, you'll happily give to those you love, but the gifts you receive are also important to you.

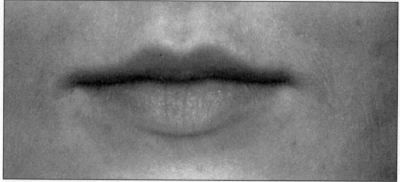

Fig. 86: A Cupid's Bow indicates a tendency to be self-indulgent.

If your lips are thin in a normal-sized mouth, you may not be very emotionally expressive and probably don't put a high priority on the touchy-feely side of life. But this feature can also be indicative of holding on to tension and stress. While you do lose some of the natural collagen in your lips as you age, it's also true that you may develop thin lips because you're holding them more tightly, compressing them due to stress. This is especially common in the type A personality. In the end, the meaning is the same: Because you're stressed, you'll be less likely to be emotionally available to your friends as well.

A very small mouth with thin lips indicates not feeling safe on many levels. The mouth is about caring, nurturing, and a safe home. If you don't feel that you'll be taken care of, you may not feel that it's safe to give to others. If no one has been tender and unselfish with you, you might not even understand how to move into the energy of generosity. You may have a great need to feel taken care of first, before you can extend that offer to someone

else. I've had many clients with extremely small mouths tell me similar stories about emotionally distant mothers; not feeling safe in the world; or never having had a stable, long-term home. This is a major Earth deficiency that appears in this kind of mouth.

You can also read how depleted your Earth may have become by looking at your mouth. Earth is about giving and caring, after all, and that's a wonderful thing. But if you extend yourself too much without getting enough nurturing, you'll become depleted, emotionally and/or physically.

Any markings, discolorations, or scarring around the mouth can be a sign of deficient Earth energy. One of my students was a single mother of four children, running her own business with a large staff to manage, and working herself into the ground. She had acne scarring around her mouth from her teenage years and was always very self-conscious about it. It was a mark of a lifelong pattern of overgiving that was destined to wear her out if she didn't pay close attention to balance, which she wasn't. By that point in her life, "all work and no play" had really taken its toll on her; she found herself exhausted and depressed. On a whim, she signed up for a spiritual-growth workshop at a beautiful retreat center. Not having ever attended this kind of course before, she joked with her staff she was "going to Venus for a week!"

She had to work so hard in advance in order to get away that she made herself ill—she arrived with a fever and worried that she'd have to spend the entire time in bed. But partly because of her own determination and also because of the healing nature of the workshop, by the next day the fever was gone, and at the end of the week, she was glowing with health and vitality. But the most important thing that happened was rediscovering the need to take care of herself and balance all her giving with self-nurturing.

Two weeks after the experience, she called to tell me a story:

My kids met me at the airport when I got home, and we went out to dinner and a movie to celebrate my being back. All night long, I kept catching my oldest son staring at me. Finally, I asked him why.

He looked startled and stammered that there was no rea-
son—he just hadn't seen me in a while. But he kept looking at
me, and as he headed to bed that night, he turned to me and
blurted out, "Mom? Can I ask you a question?"

"Of course. What is it?"

"But will you tell me the truth?" he insisted.

"Well, absolutely, honey!" I reassured him. I had no idea
what he was thinking.

"You didn't go to a workshop, did you?" he asked.

"Of course I did! What are you talking about?"

"You had plastic surgery, didn't you? Your scars are all
gone."

I ran to the mirror and sure enough, my mouth looked
normal—I could barely see any of the scarring.

In the space of one week, her appearance had radically altered.
Your face is just a mirror of your inner self. When you change on
the inside, your face evolves as well. This is how quickly shifts can
happen for someone, the internal reflected in the external. If, in
fact, my student *had* undergone plastic surgery but not experienced
the inner transformation, her scars might have been gone, but new
markings would have soon replaced them.

Upper Eyelid

The Chinese sometimes call the upper eyelid area "Assets"
because they show any issues around accumulation of some sort.
This can be positive or negative. Eyelids that are full or a bit puffy
(Fig. 87) show that you're good at saving or investing, but if the
puffiness is too great, it means excess Earth and can indicate stagnation. It can manifest as weight gain, stagnant qi in the body, or
a general "stuckness" in life.

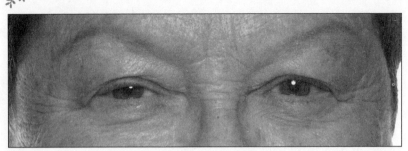

Fig. 87: Puffy upper eyelids indicate a talent for investing or saving.

Bridge of the Nose

The area at the top of your nose right between your eyes is also an Earth feature. This is the second Reservoir of Wealth on your face. (Your earlobes are the first one.) This feature is said to show how easily money comes into your life—for example, a broad bridge (Fig. 88) allows a lot of money to come through!

What this actually indicates, however, is a bigger picture, of which money is one aspect. In fact, it shows how energy flows. If the area is broad, you'll naturally have more life force coming through and thus will be able to work longer and harder, resulting in more money.

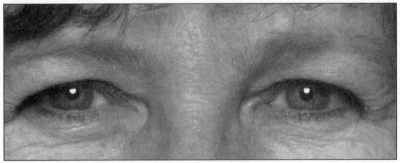

Fig. 88: A broad bridge of the nose shows a plentiful supply of energy coming through.

A narrow bridge (Fig. 89) means that the flow will be less strong. Income may be slower overall or require more work to obtain. If you have this appearance, you'll need to take greater care to protect your energy and make sure that you allow ample time for self-nurturing.

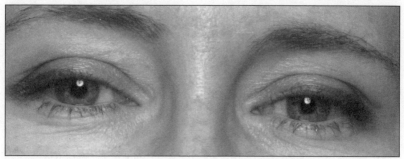

Fig. 89: A narrow bridge of the nose shows a smaller supply of energy.

It's not uncommon to see a horizontal wrinkle across the bridge of the nose (Fig. 90). This is often a sign that you have made or will make a significant life change around the age of 40. Sometimes it's a divorce, switching jobs, or a midlife crisis that stimulates some major modification in how you live.

The bridge of your nose, as an Earth feature, also mirrors your level of self-nurturing. If you've been overgiving or not receiving enough in return, your energy will be diminished. Early warning signs appear on the face in the form of small wrinkles or discoloration; an Earth imbalance will show up here even before it reveals itself at the mouth.

However, this part of the face also can show health issues. If lines, discolorations, or markings appear in this area, it could mean a digestive problem instead. And it's said that babies who have a blue line across the bridge of the nose may have food allergies.

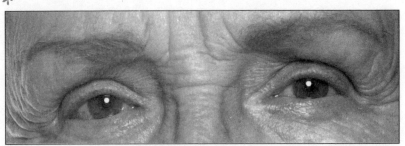

Fig. 90: A horizontal line across the bridge of the nose usually means a change at around age 40.

Area above the Upper Lip (on Either Side of the Philtrum)

The mouth and the area around it show any issues regarding nurturing, giving and receiving in life, and your expectations and disappointments in that regard. These are often difficult subjects for many people, especially women. In our culture, whether they're naturally part of Earth Element or not, most girls are socialized at an early age to learn the "mothering" energy of this Element— being the caretakers, always aware of everyone else's needs, and putting themselves last. Women who are wives and mothers have had to move into that position most deeply, but even those who choose to stay single or not have children were taught early in life to focus on taking care of others. This creates the risk of an Earth imbalance. When anyone is in a pattern of giving away too much and not taking good enough care of her own needs, things get off-kilter.

If you feel as though you've been putting too much out into the world and not getting enough caring energy back, or if it seems as though you haven't been able to get enough of what you want in life because you've had to support others, you may begin to harbor negative feelings about this experience. If so, your upper lip area may become marked or have areas of discoloration. If you continue to hold or build on this dynamic over a long period of time, your emotions can grow from simple disappointment or unhappiness into some level of resentment and bitterness. The most common indication of this is a series of tiny vertical lines on the area above your upper lip (Fig. 91). The wrinkles are a sign that you may have been too "other directed" or that you might feel that the people in your life haven't given you what you need.

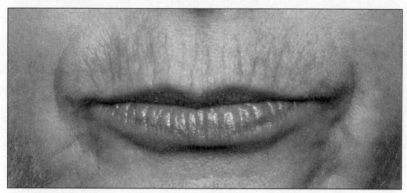

Fig. 91: Vertical lines above the upper lip show an Earth deficiency.

When you're disappointed, you'll unconsciously make a kind of pursed or pouting expression with your mouth with barely discernible muscle movements. If you continue in a pattern of this type of emotion, repeating this subtle movement in thousands of moments over time eventually engraves vertical lines into this part of your face. These are signs of disappointment, resentment, or even bitterness held in the body. You've been giving with expectations, wanting the same love that you're sending out. Unconsciously, you may feel that *you* followed the rules and did what you were expected to but ended up just sacrificing your energy and not getting enough care or gratitude in return.

Along with overgiving, another common Earth habit is not telling others what you need or want. As you recall, this Element represents the archetype of the mother, who doesn't make many personal demands on the rest of the family. She so easily intuits the things everyone else needs, but she tends to expect that they'll just naturally know to give to her in the same way. But family members usually take Mom for granted and aren't so caring in return.

So if you have these lines and feel that you haven't gotten what you need from the people in your life, it may be that you haven't

been letting them know what you want. Perhaps you've been silently expecting that it would be obvious. This isn't usually how life—or relationships—work, unfortunately. You may need to get some clarity on the situation in order to see how you can successfully make your needs known. You might also try to look at ways in which your friends and family may have been attempting to give to you. Sometimes you can be so focused on your expectations or disappointment that you run the risk of missing all the ways that they're trying to show you love.

If you haven't been receiving what you need in life, you must also allow yourself to fill that void! Self-nurturing is an important quality to learn, for once you have the ability to show love to yourself, you may not feel that others should have to provide so much. Resentful or demanding behavior can melt away, and the vertical lines may ease as well.

If you smoke, you may think that you developed these marks as a result of that habit, which can happen, but the underlying basis is still all about an Earth imbalance. Smoking actually has to do with Fire, which nourishes Earth in the Five Element cycle. So if you smoke, you may unconsciously be trying to bring more Fire qi into your life and subsequently boost your Earth. Additionally, pulling smoke into your mouth is a motion similar to eating—an Earth activity—and even the primal act of sucking involved in the habit invokes the essence of Earth, the child nursing at the mother's breast.

This Element is about giving, as you've learned, but it's also about receptivity and softness; so any activity that centers around pampering, tenderness, and comfort can replenish its energy. You must decide for yourself what you need in this regard. It might be as simple as a day at a spa, where you're totally catered to, dinners out with loving friends, or just more time to sit and read a book.

An Earth deficiency may go much deeper, however. It might have originated in a difficult relationship with your mother or whoever filled that role in your life. Or it may have been the loss of your mother at an early age, a childhood with no stable home, or unhappiness in a long-term relationship. Even in these cases, however, the same principles apply: Anything that can create softness, receptivity, compassion, and acceptance of the self and others can go a long way toward resolving Earth issues. Begin to give yourself what you need and you'll see the results in your mouth . . . and your life.

In addition, remember that this area of the face also signals digestive issues, especially in the stomach area. As always, it's important to keep in mind that any marking can indicate an emotional or physical challenge or both.

As discussed earlier, your mouth is also an indicator of what the decade of your 50s will be like. This is often the period in which markings will appear, and it's the time when the issues they represent really begin to intrude on your life. It's also important to realize that your face is giving information to everyone you meet. If you have markings of resentment on your upper lip or a downturned mouth (Fig. 92), you're telling the world: "I've been disappointed, and I'm sure it will happen again!" Life will probably oblige.

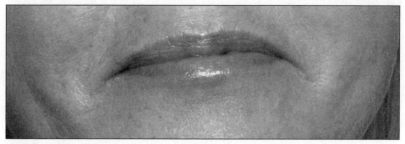

Fig. 92: A downturned mouth can reveal built-up negative feelings.

If your face shows these kinds of tendencies, it's imperative that you do some self-examination regarding any issues relating to giving and receiving. It can also be helpful to notice what your mouth feels like now and then keep monitoring it throughout the day, just like you check your rearview mirror when you drive. You'll be surprised by how many times you'll sense tension there. Consciously relax the muscles, and then give yourself the gift of a small smile. Over time, you'll find less and less need to make adjustments in this area.

Lower Cheeks near the Mouth

Plump lower cheeks in the area next to the mouth are called "moneybags" and are the third and most important Reservoir of Wealth on the face (Fig. 93); they're considered to be a sign that you can attain and hold on to wealth. It's said that you develop the bags before you get the money, so if you fit this description, you're on the right track! But of course, this area doesn't just relate to financial matters. Basically, it means that you have extra energy—an accumulation of excess qi that can sustain you.

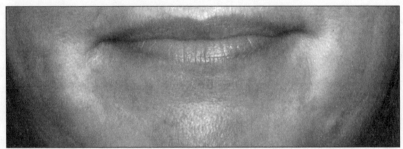

Fig. 93: The plump "moneybags" on the lower cheeks show reserves of energy.

Full lower cheeks are a sign of the wonderful Earthy quality of being able to live well and enjoy it. If you have this feature, you know how to be open to all the pleasures of life and appreciate them more fully than some others. It will probably also be important to you to have close relationships as a part of a satisfying existence. You'll excel in jobs that involve working with others, including management, because people will perceive your warm, caring nature and be happy to do what you ask. Anyone will subliminally respond in a positive way to a face with these cheeks.

Moneybags that appear plump but sagging or soft and flabby can mean that your Earth has gotten depleted. You may have become such a giver that you've developed a pattern of sacrificing too much of your power. Unfortunately, if you're stuck in this pattern, the solutions that come to mind may only involve giving more.

A client who was in her late 60s and lived alone in a small apartment had such features. Her married son owned a multi-million-dollar business; and his wife didn't work, preferring to spend most of her time shopping and redecorating their home. My client worked for her son as his office manager and was frequently in the office from 7 A.M. to 7 P.M. but earned no salary. She even made his lunch each day and was paying his mortgage to the tune of $3,300 per month. But the reason she'd come to me for a face reading was that she felt guilty about not helping him enough! She was hoping that perhaps we could discover better ways for her to support him so that he'd finally be happy. This is an example of Earth being far out of balance, giving and giving until there's nothing left to give without realigning the energy.

Earth is about giving, but also about receiving. This Element needs to care for others in order to feel happy, but a common lesson for everyone who has this energy is to be able to also open their arms and accept the same warm love they're so good at bestowing upon others.

There's also a particular face and body type that reveals another specific kind of Earth personality that holds more stuckness than some others. This person has less roundness to her face and body than most in this Element. Instead, she's more blockish and especially broad through the upper and middle torso. Even her face is slightly more square than round and can be a bit heavier in the lower part, around the jowls or jaw area. Her chin may be strong, but with an extra plumpness; and she'll tend to have a large, imposing energy, even if she's not tall. Former First Lady Barbara Bush is a classic example.

This shows strong and powerful Earth energy, definitely the kind of person you want on your side because she can get things accomplished where others will fail. But if her energy falls out of balance, there's a danger that she'll become stuck in resentment, sometimes verging on anger. She's opinionated and resistant to change, and as a result, can be controlling and overbearing. She probably has the vertical lines above her upper lip that show resentment and bitterness, or her mouth will be turned down tightly.

She's still a caring person, and in fact has gone into imbalance by giving too much. In her attempt to rebalance, she has become stubborn and controlling. She tells everyone what to do in every way she can and resists doing what others ask. I often see this body type in the women who were part of the first wave of high-level corporate executives. They probably achieved success in part due to their strong ability to push their own agenda on others and their resistance to challenge.

This Earth personality still has that deep desire and ability to help, but it's often overwhelmed by her feelings of resentment and even victimization. She's the one who may offer to assist you but then not come through as promised. She truly does want to lend a hand; but in the end, her core feeling of having been the victim will take hold and she'll feel that too much has been asked of her already. It can be difficult to see her through compassionate eyes, but her behavior is really just due to her Elemental suffering—her desire for love and appreciation.

Earth: Who Are You? What Is Your Calling?

Who are you, and how can you fall in love with who you really are? How can you clear the way for your true calling to emerge? You must first allow your Earth essence to flourish in order to manifest your purpose in the world. If this is your Element, your true nature needs a strong connection with others. Your reason for being is the fulfillment that relationships bring you, and people will be at the center of everything you do. Invest your energy in finding good companions on your journey because they'll be the ones who will make your life worth living. Allow yourself to give to and support others in both your professional and personal life, as that will feed your soul. Recognize that the balanced cycle of giving includes the ability to open your arms and receive the same wonderful affection that you give so freely.

Find ways to use your greatest strengths: caring, kindness, patient diplomacy, and most of all your desire to help everyone be fully nurtured. Don't deny your need to go down your path arm in arm with those you love. Accept your desire for comfort and safety, and create a life that allows that stability. When your Earth qi is flowing, everything will come into balance, and you can encounter new possibilities beyond your wildest dreams.

Chapter 13

METAL—TO REFINE

In this chapter, I'll introduce the basics of the Metal Element, and you'll learn how to identify it. To begin, here's a quick-reference list of Metal characteristics:

- **Energy:** inward moving, contracting, hardening, evening, late fall, old age

- **Qualities:** sensitive, aware, idealistic, visionary, anxious, critical, stingy, inflexible, desires authenticity, perfectionistic, arrogant, proud, aloof, authoritative, regal, gracious, charming, ethereal, hypersensitive, self-conscious, inner sense of lack, grief, suffering

- **Major features:** nose, cheeks, pale skin, moles

- **Organs:** lungs, skin, large intestines

- **Sense organ:** nose

What to Look for

You don't need to have *all* of the following aspects for this Element to play a strong role in your life—any of these will indicate that it's a factor in your personality. The more of them you possess, the more Metal there is in your nature:

- Large nose
- Prominent upper cheeks
- Concave or lined lower cheeks
- Wide spaces between features
- Fine bone structure, small wrists and ankles
- Graceful, regal bearing
- Hypermetabolism, tend to be slim
- Pale complexion for racial heritage

Fig. 94: Metal Face

Fig. 95: Metal Face

How do you know if this is a major part of your personality? You look for your strongest features—what "speaks" to you most in your face. You may not have all or even many of these kinds of features, but if you have a sizeable nose or large upper cheeks, you have this Element in your makeup. The more strong Metal features you have, the more of this energy you have in your personality.

Well-known faces that show this Element include: Michelle Pfeiffer, Nancy Reagan, Lyle Lovett, Meryl Streep, and Adrien Brody.

If you're a typical Metal, you may have prominent upper cheeks or a large nose. You could have pale skin and tiny bones that are apparent in your petite wrists and ankles. The features on your face could be described as "sculpted," and there may be broader spaces between each feature than in other Elements. You hold yourself with a natural regality that some people perceive as arrogance or aloofness. If you have all of these characteristics, which is rare, you'll know that you're a very Metallic person!

The Personality of Metal

This Element has to do with late autumn, when the trees are letting go of their leaves, revealing tiny branches etched against the sky. Harvest time is over, and the food is being stored for the year; supplies are used frugally so there will be enough to last through the winter. Metal is the late afternoon as you clean off your desk, preparing to end your workday and retire for the evening. It's old age, when you feel the need to finish up and refine the last details as you approach the end of your life, letting go of what no longer has purpose.

The power here is the breath as it draws in the Divine source, but it's also about letting go. Energy can't enter your life if you don't move in the rhythm of holding and then releasing, always clearing space for the new to come in.

Metal calls us to refine our vision, bring clarity to our lives, and hone our goals to those that are the most meaningful and valuable for us. Its power is in its sensitivity and awareness of the fine and subtle nuances of life. The verb for this Element is "to refine." These people constantly seek perfection in all aspects of life.

If this is your Element, you're highly aware. You are the visionary, the leader, the one who can see the big picture and the fine details at the same time. The energy is associated with the archetype of the Father, and Metal often shows up as an authority who can take the mantle of power and lead the world to new horizons.

Yet this high level of sensitivity can lead to challenges. More than anyone else, you're affected by the energy of environments and the people around you, whether you're conscious of it or not, because of your tendency to have permeable personal boundaries. You're almost a "psychic sponge," due to your predisposition to soak up so many of the vibrations around you. This is often an enormous challenge—if the person who sits down next to you is stressed, you may find yourself suddenly feeling anxious or unwell, without understanding why. When you walk into a room where a bad argument took place two days earlier, you can be influenced by the residue of emotion that remains. But since this is all invisible and subtle, you'll probably have no idea that it's happening. The result is that you can end up feeling tense or stressed most of the time and blaming yourself for it.

If you recall the fairy tale "The Princess and the Pea," where only the princess is aware of the tiny pea under dozens of mattresses, you'll have an accurate picture of your Elemental temperament! The psychological term "Highly Sensitive Person" is an equivalent. You're considered to have a more finely tuned nervous system that can result in your being challenged by the onslaught of so much stimuli.

We're all walking through a sea of energy or "information" as we go about our everyday lives. And we all unconsciously read it and are affected by it. People have vibrational fields that extend out from their physical bodies, and environments also can hold the energy of what happened there. Most of us aren't conscious that our systems are reacting in this way, even though everyone has experienced knowing who's calling when the phone rings, thinking of someone right before his e-mail arrives, or even walking into a room and suddenly feeling uncomfortable for no obvious reason— only to find out later that something unpleasant had happened there. But if you're Metal, you can seem to be stuck wide open, taking in so much of this energy that you can be severely affected by it sometimes. As one student told me, "It's all too loud." He didn't mean literally noisy, but rather that the cacophony of information was just too much for his system.

In our culture, there's little language or training for how to cope with such an extreme level of sensitivity. Because of this, Metal can become overwhelmed very easily amid the relentless onslaught. If this is your Element, you may sometimes feel as if you're hovering partly out of your body because it's too difficult to be fully present and feel so much. You're probably the one who can't stay long at a busy shopping mall or who dislikes large parties, since the energy of so many people crowded around you can even be physically painful.

Because you're so sensitive, little things can bother you, and this tendency shows up in a variety of ways. You may need to have lots of time alone in order to recover from the stress of other people around you, or things must be "just so" in your environment. You won't be able to resist straightening a picture hanging slightly crooked on the wall, and you'll be the one to wipe smudges off a windowpane. One of my students said that he has to make sure the seams on all the lampshades are turned to the wall before he can feel comfortable in any room. This behavior is merely because as a Metal, he's so easily made uncomfortable by what's "off" around him, even tiny details. Similarly, you'll try to make sure things are as balanced and perfect as they can possibly be. At its extreme, this tendency manifests in obsessive-compulsive disorder, as Metal desperately tries to control the smallest aspects of everything in life in order to find some level of comfort.

Because of these needs, you can be misperceived by others as being picky, controlling, or trying to have power over someone. Without the proper understanding, it's easy for two people to get caught up in a cycle of reaction. This was illustrated by a mother and her nine-year-old daughter who came to see me for a private consultation. The woman had made the appointment in the hopes that it could help resolve a problem between them that had gotten so bad that the girl didn't even want to be around her mother anymore. Although neither one of them shared the details right away, I could tell by one look at the daughter what it might be. Her facial features, complexion, and even body type and bone structure told me all I needed to know: Metal.

I explained the daughter's personality and needs, describing what the girl's behavior was likely to be—that she was extremely affected by small things, even how her clothes felt on her skin could make her uncomfortable, and she might have very precise needs for bedtime rituals or food. She probably got upset if little things were moved or changed. Overall, she'd be more anxious about the details of life than other children.

Her mother's face just lit up as I spoke and she excitedly said this was exactly the problem. I was giving her an opportunity to see things in a whole new light, rather than viewing the "pickiness" as a power play. She thought it was her job as a parent to teach her daughter respect, and she'd interpreted the attempts at control as a way of trying to seize authority. For instance, the girl wanted the bedroom door left exactly halfway open at night, but my client refused because she felt it was important to have the final say. However, her daughter cried terribly about the door position—not because she was trying to take charge, but because only that exact setup made her feel safe and able to sleep.

Another conflict between them was the mother's tendency to be a bit disorganized and run late, which meant that she often didn't make time to warn her daughter that they only had five minutes before they had to leave the house on an errand. The Metal personality needs time to prepare, and rushing made the girl highly anxious, so she became upset when her mother urged her to hurry. Again, my client had looked at this as a power play, but now she understood her daughter's personal need for space to breathe and time to adjust to a new idea.

A week after our meeting, I got a happy phone call. Just this new awareness had improved things so drastically that the little girl was actually wanting to spend as much time with her mom as possible! There was a new relaxed warmth between them, thanks to this woman's ability to accept a new understanding of her daughter's nature, needs, and behavior.

Unsurprisingly, Metal is probably the most difficult Element to live with. You can indeed become hypersensitive, anxious, perfectionistic, and even critical and controlling as you react to any imbalance around you. Part of the beauty of viewing yourself through the language of the Five Elements is to be able to see these traits as not just yours alone, but as a type of energy. This allows you to find space to understand your nature and how others may experience you.

And what might be called your biggest weakness is also your greatest strength. Your sensitivity is an incredible talent in many ways—for instance, you can be a charming and compassionate chameleon with people, elegantly reading their "frequencies" and knowing how to adjust to their needs in any interaction in order to make them comfortable. With your strong awareness of how

things "feel," you can create exquisite beauty in any environment or achieve great success in projects due to your care with the finest nuances. You're so attuned to what's happening on many levels in any situation and able to see far into the future to anticipate problems that you can discern more powerful and sustainable solutions than most people. You can use your energy to great advantage if you can learn how to stay in balance.

Superficial relationships and small talk don't interest you. As Metal, you're driven toward finding a meaningful life that's rich with a sense of purpose—even an authentic connection with the sacred in some way, although you might not define yourself as a spiritual person. You have high standards and won't be very comfortable in the company of people who don't share your strong sense of ethics.

This Element is precise and analytical, with great attention to detail; you're the one who'll immediately find the typo in a letter. You'll want to do things correctly, first and foremost, and care greatly about the quality of your work. You'll also tend to be so conscientious and anxious about getting everything right that you may become easily upset over small problems. For instance, running late isn't a Metal quality! If you find you're tardy to an appointment, you may arrive feeling very nervous and stressed.

Overall, you'll be highly self-critical. The worst thing someone can do to you is to offer some "constructive criticism." You're already so tough on yourself that knowing someone else noticed when you did something wrong can be too much to bear. What's worse is that Metal also has a very hard time letting any praise in because your harsh inner voice can be so strong.

The Element is sometimes called the Perfect Host, and you're charming, gracious, and highly attentive to the subtleties of any social interaction. You value manners; fairness and following rules are important to you. You may always bring a gift when invited to dinner and might be more upset than others by someone who commits a social gaffe. But because the nature of Metal is to harden, you can become too tight about rules and regulations.

One friend was teaching her highly Metal teenage daughter to drive. During their first foray onto the freeway, the girl knew that the speed limit was 65 miles per hour, so she nervously but duti-fully accelerated. Soon, however, traffic got thicker and began to slow down to about 40, but the girl was so fixated on obeying the rule that she should drive the posted speed that she raced forward until finally her mother had to shriek, *"Brake!"* as they rapidly approached the rear end of a truck!

Metal and the Material

Because this Elemental energy also has to do with letting go, you probably enjoy getting rid of what's no longer necessary. It may be important to you to finish each day with a clear desk or to spend a Sunday afternoon cleaning out your cupboards. The best friend any woman can have is a Metal who wears the same size as she does. Her friend will frequently go through her closet and pass along what she no longer wants!

Not being attached to "stuff" is a good quality, but of course this can be taken too far. There's sometimes a Metal tendency to let go of too much—to do without, contracting to the point of self-deprivation. This can manifest in many different ways, such as living an ascetic lifestyle, being too solitary, or being extremely frugal about money or food intake.

Years ago, I had a very Metal personal assistant who lived with me and ate very, very little. She'd gone through a system of spiritual training that was known for teaching people to develop the ability to practically live without food. She said that she wanted to walk very lightly upon the earth and take as little as possible from it, but it was really a severe deprivation of her own body.

She worked with me for more than a year, and when she finally left, it was only because she'd heard about a new course of train-ing that she dearly wanted to experience. There was a teacher who claimed to show you how to control your body temperature so perfectly that you'd need to own only one piece of clothing and would never be too hot or cold!

This demonstrates an extreme Metal imbalance: the desire to control perfectly, and to *not* be in the body if at all possible because

so much stimulation is overwhelming when your sensitivity is out of control. But I believe that the lesson for this Element is learning to fully come *into* the physical, not the other way around. It's often uncomfortable to feel as much as you do, and the desire to get away from all that "information" is understandable. But to have chosen the gift of living as a human on this beautiful earth and then trying to deny the full experience seems to me a terrible mistake. With your high awareness, you can learn to have an exquisitely beautiful time while fully present.

The Chinese symbol for the Metal Element is a coin, which has two sides. There is a dual nature here: great wealth and utter simplicity, lofty ideals and petty details, pride and humility. If you're Metal, this duality can show up in your life. You may have the tendency to self-deprive and live an extremely simple existence, or you can end up in great opulence, or experience both in your life. You might be aristocratic and have high self-esteem or be very self-effacing and shy. You could value the ways of the past and long for the good old days, or your mind may be far out in space, focusing on the future, reading science fiction, or working with the latest in technology. Notice any aspects of this dual nature in yourself if this is your Element.

Metal Style

— **Clothing:** You'll love simple, classic designs; very refined styles; and soft fabrics, because the feel on your skin is of utmost importance. You don't like heavy, bulky, or rough clothing. You especially gravitate to fabrics such as silk and cashmere—not because you're snooty, but because they feel so lovely. Plastic-feeling polyesters or itchy labels on the back of your neck will be unbearable. Colors will be calm; if not monochromatic, they'll tend toward whites, grays, or pastels. If the fabric has a metallic sheen to it, all the better.

If you're a Metal woman, you probably love real jewels. Even if you can only afford one strand of real pearls, you'll prefer that over heaps of costume jewelry. Your shoes, like all the rest of your clothing, will be as perfect as possible!

— **Home:** Minimalism and spaciousness will be the order of the day, with a palette of pale neutrals or a monochromatic scheme. This allows your highly sensitive system to feel as relaxed as possible— Metal doesn't need the stimulation that Fire craves! Your goal is to have a perfectly harmonious balance of beautiful things around you. Because you tend to be claustrophobic, you'll like larger rooms that help you feel able to take a full breath. You like to see far and may have large picture windows that allow distant views, with your home preferably sited above the landscape, rather than level with it. Space and cleanliness are of utmost importance.

Metal is more affected by visual clutter than any other Element, but this doesn't mean that you're a total neat freak. Open any drawer or closet, and you may find a chaos of confusion. How things look on the surface is what matters most to you; as long as you can close the closet doors and hide the mess, you'll be fine!

It's often the Metal person who brings me in for feng shui since she can feel when something is "off" in the energy of her environment. I'm greeted with enormous sighs of relief when I validate her sense, as everyone else in the family thinks she's crazy!

— **Movement:** Anything that encourages rhythmic breathing will be beneficial, such as running, walking, aerobics, yoga, and swimming. You aren't attracted to rough or competitive activities, especially team sports.

— **Profession:** Because of your fine-tuned awareness of beauty, you can excel in fashion, interior, or graphic design. Your precision and care also create success in professions such as surgeon, software designer, accountant, editor, and artist. And because of your heightened sensitivity, you may end up working with subtle energy in a career such as feng shui, space clearing, or energy medicine.

Perhaps you've recognized yourself or a friend in the descriptions above, and it may have given you new insights and awareness. But you may feel that while you see *some* Metal, it doesn't completely describe you or your friend. Remember that while we all have some of each of the five Elements in our personalities, usually

one or two are emphasized—some people even have four of the Elements strongly in their faces and are weak in only one. So it may be that as you read this book, you can identify a second, third, or even fourth category that gives you a complete understanding of who you are inside.

But even if you don't find Metal features emphasized in your face, you still have a nose, cheeks, and so on! In the next chapter, we'll examine each of these features individually and learn what they can tell us in more detail about how Metal manifests in your inherent spirit.

Chapter 14

READING THE METAL FEATURES

As I've mentioned, in addition to giving the entire face a certain look, each Element corresponds with specific facial features. In this chapter, you'll learn how to gain even more insight into the Metal Element from each of these body parts.

Nose

Remember that in face reading, you judge the size of a feature by comparing it to the size of the rest of the features on your face; what's large on one person might be small on another. Additionally, you always read within races: You compare Caucasian faces to other Caucasians, African to African, Asian to Asian, and so on. You can read mixed-race faces, too; it just takes a little more practice.

The nose is the major indicator of Metal on the face and represents the capacity for power. The larger it is, the greater this potential. It's said that in ancient times in the Middle East, the noses of the young princes were pulled and massaged because they believed that no one could be king without a sizable nose. If this feature is big, it also shows ambition and independence; very large ones are signs of a potentially egotistical and self-centered personality. And if your nose sticks out very far—more than one inch from your face—it's a sign that you're a trailblazer. So getting a "nose job" can not only diminish your potential life experience in your 40s, as I mentioned earlier, but it can impact your lifelong personal power.

A flatter or smaller nose is an indication that you're not so focused on your power in the world. You're more content and less worried about achievement. You probably excel in team situations and don't feel the need to stand out as special.

A nose doesn't have to be large to carry one kind of Metal essence. If it's perfectly formed, it's the mark of the Metal quality of being an idealist (Fig. 96). You give importance to your vision and desire to live a meaningful life.

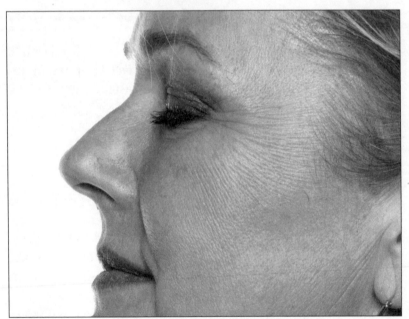

Fig. 96: A classic, perfectly formed Metal nose is the sign of an idealist.

A bony nose (Fig. 97) indicates an ascetic personality, someone not so interested in material things. If you have this feature, you may take Metal idealism further—for instance, you won't be interested in a career just for the money. You'll give your ideals priority over comfort in life.

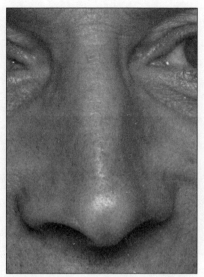

Fig. 97: A bony nose reflects less interest in material things.

If you have a dramatically bony, narrow nose, you have the potential to take this to the extreme. You may be disdainful of money, can actually be attracted to hardship, and will resist pleasure.

A "ski slope" or turned-up nose is the sign of a sentimental person (Fig. 98). You may also be more free with your money, giving it away easily, but you'll tend to get it back again in some way. This generosity includes affection—you're very caring and need to have affection returned.

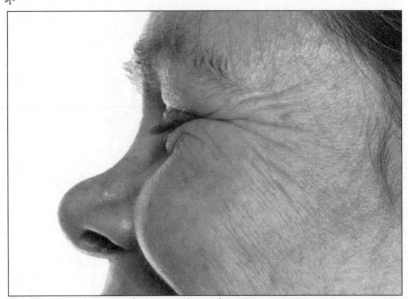

Fig. 98: A turned-up nose shows a sentimental temperament.

A bump on your nose just below the bridge (Fig. 99) shows that you have a deep need to be in charge somehow, and you may feel dissatisfied if you aren't. It usually shows up as an almost irresistible impulse to tell others what to do or how to do it that stems from the knowledge that you're more aware of all the details in any situation—which is probably true! The difficulty comes from common Metal issues: boundaries and control. It's not always appropriate to be the one who takes charge. If you have this kind of nose, knowing this may really help you understand your feelings and behavior. You may already recognize this tendency in your personality or have experienced people reacting badly when you feel that you're just trying to help. Again, like all qualities, this one isn't negative or positive; it's just a part of your nature that's important to understand.

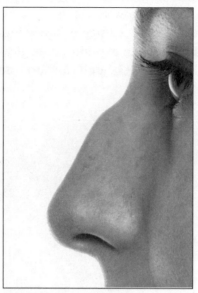

Fig. 99: A bump just below the bridge of the nose shows the need to be in charge.

I once consulted for a company where one particular staff member was creating stress for most of the others. This man was part of a team working on a very important project, but he constantly tried to run the show. He attempted to control staff meetings, commanded others to take on special tasks, and ordered individual colleagues to do as he said. The more they resisted, the angrier and more upset he became, until no one wanted to work with him at all. Management was on the verge of firing him but really didn't want to because he was so highly skilled.

When I interviewed him, at first I couldn't discern why he might be acting this way, aside from his prominent nose. It wasn't until he took off his glasses and turned in profile that I saw what had been hidden—the very large bump on the bridge of his nose. This explained it for me: He had an inherent need to have authority over someone. If this happened, he'd feel much more satisfied and calm down. My advice wasn't to fire him, but instead to change his job slightly and give him an assistant to order around!

Other types of noses show subtle differences in personality. A downturned nose (Fig. 100) is a sign of shrewdness. This can show up in a variety of ways, from excelling strategically in your job to seeing behind others' motives, but it can also contribute to a sense of overall skepticism.

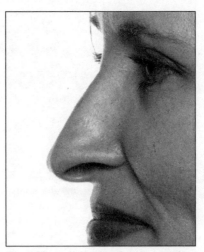

Fig. 100: A downturned nose reveals a shrewd nature.

However, if the downturned tip of your nose extends down to cover part of your philtrum (Fig. 101), your cleverness will extend to finances. It's said to indicate someone who can hold on to money and manage it well. The deeper meaning of this feature is being prudent about how you invest your energy in all aspects of life.

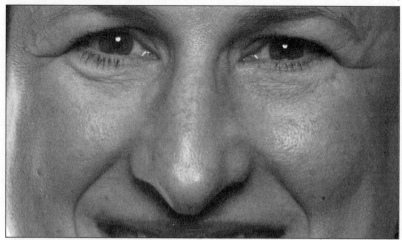

Fig. 101: A downturned nose that covers part of the philtrum shows skill with investments.

A fleshier nose (Fig. 102) indicates a little additional Earth Element in your energy. This means that you're happy living in the material world and like your comforts and pleasures. Collectors and gourmands often have this feature.

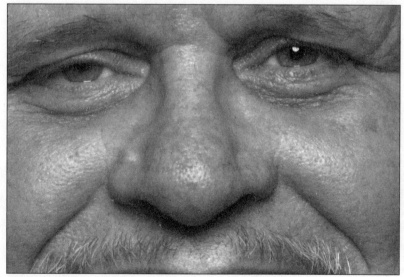

Fig. 102: A fleshier nose indicates enjoyment of material pleasures.

Nostrils

Chinese face reading teaches that the nostrils show how money is spent, but it's really about how you spend energy of *any* sort, including cash. If you have large nostrils, you'll feel easier about dispensing funds and also about putting your "all" into a project. You may have an inherent, unconscious trust that there will be plenty more where that came from; or you'll be living a life where you know you'll have a steady flow of abundance, such as having a steady job or a paid-off mortgage. But this appearance can also be a sign that there's a danger of spending too freely—with money, energy, time, or all of the above.

However, if you can see directly into your nostrils while looking at your face straight on (Fig. 103), this definitely indicates that this could be a problem. And if you see this feature on your client, you'll need to have strong integrity in your dealings with him, as he may be an "easy mark," willing to buy whatever you have to offer. Fortunately, this feature is often modified or controlled by some other aspect of the face; for instance, large earlobes would indicate that he does keep future needs in mind and will always be financially stable.

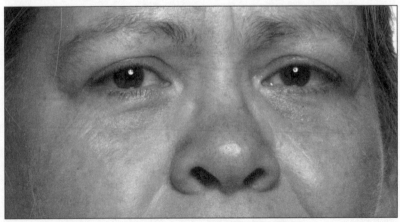

Fig. 103: Nostrils that are highly visible indicate free spending with money and energy.

Small nostrils show that you will tend to hold on to your money or energy. You'll be aware of how much something costs (financially or energetically) and are careful about how much you're willing to give in order to have it. You'll be much more discerning about what you choose to spend for. Long and narrow nostrils signify that you're a bargain hunter; you want value for your money.

I once had a student who was a philanthropist, well known for his generosity. He had surgery for a deviated septum that also changed the shape of his nostrils so that they became much narrower. Soon after the operation, he decided to stop giving so freely to charities!

In terms of the physical body, the nose mirrors the health of the back. Although this may sound strange, Chinese face reading teaches that the condition of this feature is a direct reflection of the state of the spine. In the beginning of my studies, my highly skeptical nature found this hard to swallow, and I still check the connection in every consultation I do. For instance, when I see a nose where the bone curves to one side, I often find that the client has scoliosis, with the spine swerving in the same pattern as the nose (Fig. 104).

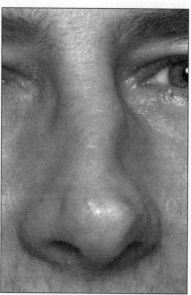

Fig. 104: The nose is considered to be a mirror of the spine.

Even if scoliosis isn't a problem, if there's an odd bend to some-one's nose, I'll often hear that he has chronic back problems. A few of my students had polio early in life, were temporarily paralyzed, and still have weakness in their spines. They all showed strong markings on their noses, too.

The upper nose reflects the health of the neck and upper back, the middle of the nose corresponds to the midback, and the lower nose shows the condition of the lower back. Variation in the bone or cartilage of the nose relates to spinal problems, while irregularity in the flesh of this feature relates to muscular trouble in the back.

One elderly student had a very large nose, and the tip was disfigured and discolored as well. He'd struggled with mysterious chronic back pain all his life, and it continued to go undiagnosed. His mother had told him that he'd fallen out of his crib onto his face as a child and ended up with a severe bend in his nose. As a teenager, he'd had surgery to correct it, and while it did result in a straighter nose, something else seemed to have gone wrong during the operation or perhaps in the healing process. The end of his nose became discolored and malformed, as if the blood supply wasn't flowing correctly. He recalled that after his time in the hospital, his back pain mysteriously became much more severe and continued for the rest of his life.

Cheeks

If you have prominent upper cheeks (Fig. 105), you have the Metal ability to hold authority. This quality can be positive in many ways. You say what you need and communicate what's required in any situation. You can run a business or a household, giving orders as necessary. Strong cheeks can, however, show a tendency to be bossy—or at least the need to share your opinions with others! If your cheeks are rounded with some extra padding, this can soften the effect and add Earthy warmth. In this case, people will be happy to do what you tell them because they feel the caring energy behind your words.

Fig. 105: Prominent cheeks show the ability to speak with authority and state what you need.

You'll sometimes see that the actual bones of the cheeks are especially prominent at the back of the face, toward the ears. Occasionally, the cheekbones will protrude so strongly in this area that they almost seem to connect to the ears. This can indicate a bit of ruthlessness, especially if the front of the cheeks aren't rounded. This characteristic can show up in a range of ways, from simply a sarcastic style of humor all the way to cruelty in the pursuit of power. It also means that if these people make a promise, they'll be likely to keep it; in the same way, if they give you an ultimatum, you should believe them!

Flat cheeks (Fig. 106) indicate that you don't enjoy having to tell others what to do; neither do you like being "bossed" in any aspect of life. You prefer to work on your own, dislike being supervised, and may have self-esteem issues or lack confidence in your accomplishments. If you have these cheeks in combination with eyebrows that come close together in the middle, as discussed in the chapter on the Wood Element, you'll probably be happier in situations where you won't be micromanaged. You'll do best where you've got the freedom to choose your own tasks and don't have to supervise others.

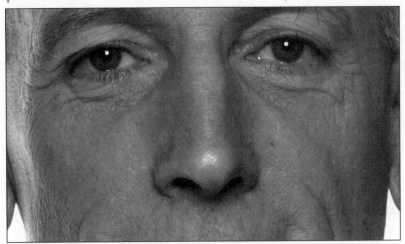

Fig. 106: Flatter cheeks reveal a dislike of being supervised or overseeing others.

You may notice one or more small curved wrinkles directly under your eyes (Fig. 107). These are a sign that you've experienced a painful emotional loss at some point in your life. They often represent losing someone who meant a lot to you—the ending of a relationship, for instance, or even a death.

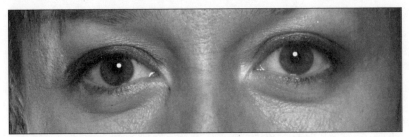

Fig. 107: Small curved lines under the eyes show an emotional loss.

However, if sorrow from a loss is impacting your life in a significant way, lines will also appear on your cheeks (Fig. 108). And if the event has a deep and lasting influence in your life, the marks will grow longer, moving down onto your lower cheeks to become "grief lines." This doesn't mean that something is wrong with you; these emotions are a natural part of life. Experiencing grief and loss is a part of the energy of Metal, and we all have this essence in our spirits. However, if you find yourself holding on to these feelings so much that you're not able to move forward in life, this inability to let go can be reflected by deep lines down your cheeks.

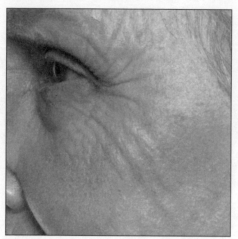

Fig. 108: Lines that extend onto the cheeks indicate feelings of sorrow.

Any wrinkle, marking, or discoloration on your cheeks could indicate an emotional issue to do with Metal. They reflect anything related to your feelings of sorrow and grief or your sense of personal authority and your ability to express it. But a mark can also correspond to a specific incident in the year of life indicated on the facial map provided earlier in the book (see pages 42 and 43). Because this area can also show the health of the lungs, it may also relate to a health issue; or all of the above can factor into its meaning.

Lower Cheeks

The area below the cheekbones reveals the effects of stress on emotional and physical health. When there are issues such as overwork, undereating, shallow breathing, suffering that's gone on too long, or feeling bereft or that you're lacking something, they'll show up here as "hollowness" or vertical creases down the sides of your lower cheeks. These are called "lack lines" (Fig. 109), a sign

of Metal in your nature, and indicate that something's missing in life—that is, whether it's material or emotional, something isn't "enough."

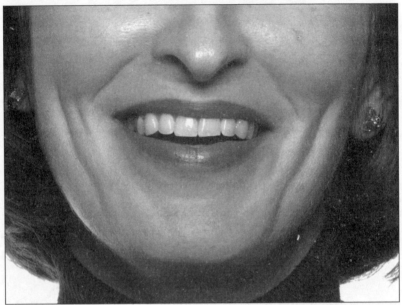

Fig. 109: Lack lines can be a symptom of stress or a lifelong sense of scarcity.

If these vertical lines are permanently engraved in your cheeks, it can be a sign that you didn't feel well loved and nurtured, probably early in life; or perhaps you grew up in poverty and still carry that consciousness into adult life. These lines can also develop if you're going down the Metal path of self-deprivation. You may be doing without or working too hard without factoring in time for rest and comfort. You could also be concerned about your financial stability and feel anxious about spending money. If this imbalance continues over the long run, the end result can be a deep belief that there isn't enough for you and you aren't safe—and if that's the case, then it follows that you won't feel that you have sufficient resources to share with others. In such a frame of mind, it's nearly impossible to be truly relaxed or giving.

When the lines are quite deep or the entire area has become very hollow, this feeling has been taken to the extreme. Billionaire

J. Paul Getty's face was a good example of this feature. He had vast wealth, yet he installed pay phones in his enormous mansion because he didn't want to foot the bill for his guests' calls!

Lack lines can develop temporarily when you've been overdoing it and your system is stressed, and Metal people often tend to get at least faint marks of this kind showing up now and then. They can be a good indicator that you need to rest, and perhaps see if you need to soften your attitude toward yourself—and life in general.

The sorrow and grief lines discussed earlier can grow longer to turn into lack lines over time. Such an occurrence is a sign that you may be holding on to your emotions so much that your loss has created a huge emptiness in your life. If this feeling is so deep and lasting that it's become a major influence, it may be important for you to summon Metal's ability to let go.

Fa Lin Lines

These are the two lines that eventually develop on most people's faces, running from the nose to either side of the mouth (Fig. 110). In Chinese, *fa lin* is literally translated as "orders of law." Living according to your own inner "laws" is a Metal imperative, a strong need to live an authentic and meaningful life. But for those of any Element, fa lin lines will appear when you're following your purpose. They show that your true inner authority is emerging, and are a positive marking. Unfortunately, our society usually looks upon them as a sign of age, and women often consider plastic surgery to make them disappear. I love to see people's faces light up when they discover the real meaning!

Fig. 110: The wrinkles that come down from the nose to the mouth are a sign of living in accordance with your purpose.

It's actually the *absence* of fa lin lines after the age of 50 that's worrisome. If you haven't developed them by that point, it's time to get started! It's not uncommon for women, especially, to stay in a pattern of denial of their need to "come into their own." They're often taking care of everyone else and putting their own lives last, but ignoring your purpose will eventually create an emotional and spiritual imbalance in your system. After many years, this can become a physical issue as well. It isn't healthy to suppress or deny your purpose.

Fa lin lines can show up at any age, from childhood on. I've seen very young actors who already have them deeply engraved because they've discovered their calling in life at an early age. It's also possible to have this feature but still feel as if you haven't yet quite found your purpose in life. They don't necessarily have anything to do with your career, nor do they mean that you have life all figured out! They do indicate, however, that in some important way, you're doing what you're meant to do in this lifetime.

There can be changes to the fa lin lines even after they've developed. If they grow deeper, it can indicate that you've moved more fully into your truth. Sometimes they can fork, or double lines can appear, which means that you've acquired dual purposes.

But if you see your fa lin lines become very deep in a short period of time, it can actually be the result of an Earth depletion. In this case, what will happen is that the front lower cheeks—the Earthy moneybags—are sagging slightly, creating what looks like a deeper purpose line. Instead, it may mean that you've been overgiving and need to rejuvenate your Earth by doing some self-nurturing.

The Space Between Features: Eyelids and Upper Brow

Metal people often have wider spaces between each feature. One place where this is especially meaningful is between your eyes and eyebrows. If you look straight at your face with your eyes open and can see your upper eyelids, this is another subtle sign that you have some of this Element in your personality (Fig. 111).

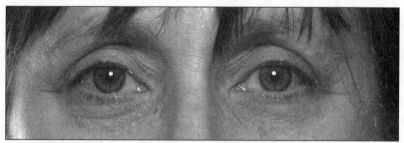

Fig. 111: Visible upper eyelids are a sign of Metal in the temperament.

If you have very large and visible upper eyelids (sometimes called "hooded"), they're considered an important aspect of your personality. This appearance indicates that a pattern of Metal grief and suffering may in some way be a significant part of your makeup; it can show an inherent tendency to suffer in a way typical of this Element during difficult times. For instance, when you're in emotional distress, you may deprive yourself of food, rest, or comfort. Your Metal energy can hold on to an issue and increase the suffering, making it too pervasive in your life.

Another place to evaluate the meaning of Metal "space between features" in this part of the face is how much room there is between your upper eyelid and your eyebrow. The larger this area is, the greater the need to maintain a safe distance from new people or situations—typical of sensitive Metal (Fig. 112). You can look and act quite aloof at times, and other people may judge you as arrogant or conceited. This isn't true; it's just another sign of your higher level of sensitivity and the need to take time in becoming comfortable with new experiences or people.

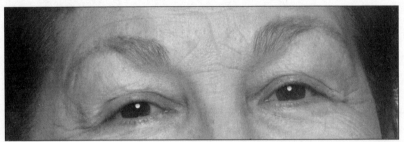

Fig. 112: High eyebrows reflect sensitivity and the need for distance from too much stimulation.

Moles

Believe it or not, Chinese face reading considers anything that sticks out on the face a sign of good luck! So most moles are a sign of "extra luck," as long as they're a healthy light or pink color. (Flat brown marks don't fall into this category.) Moles are considered extra Metal no matter where they appear on your face and are a sign of enhanced power in the meaning of that feature.

A mole on the chin (Fig. 113) indicates extra willpower and, of course, corresponding stubbornness. This is a sign of extraordinary tenacity. If you have a mole on your chin, you can succeed through sheer determination, and you may find that you've needed to call on this Watery strength to make it through certain times in your life. It's also a sign of extra Water intuitive ability. This is a talent you shouldn't underestimate; it's one of your greatest powers.

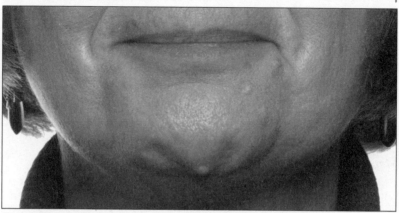

Fig. 113: A mole on the chin can mean extra willpower and intuitive ability.

A mole near the mouth (Fig. 114) shows extra Earth—increased energy associated with the enjoyment of the pleasures of life such as food, friends, and/or sex!

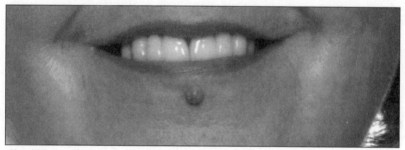

Fig. 114: A mole near the mouth shows enhanced enjoyment of the pleasures of life.

If there's a mole in the Seat of the Stamp in the brow bone, this is both positive and negative. It shows potential for great power and bodes very well for your career because it's extra qi to do with your professional ambition and drive. But it's considered unlucky for marriage since it also implies that you may be so focused on your success or have such issues about control and authority that it could affect your personal relationships. Actor Russell Crowe has this feature, along with a strong brow bone, indicating a very strong drive and issues with aggression. Although I know nothing about his personal life aside from a few comments in the news, it

does seem that the qualities I can see in his face may have had a lot to do with his success as a performer, as well as some of the legal trouble he's gotten himself into.

Any mole that's hidden, such as in the eyebrow or hair is considered to be extremely "lucky"—a very powerful sign that you have the potential for great success.

Metal: Who Are You? What Is Your Calling?

Who are you, and how can you fall in love with who you really are? How can you clear the way for your true calling to emerge? You must first allow your Metal essence to flourish in order to manifest your purpose in the world. If this is your Element, your true nature comprises very finely tuned energy. You must respect your sensitivity and not blame yourself for it because it's your path to great success in life. Recognize that your awareness of the subtle details of everything around you gives you the ability to create beauty, peace, and perfection for yourself and others. Allow yourself the time alone that you need, and understand that your system may require space and quiet to successfully release daily stress.

Find ways to use your greatest strengths: your sensitivity, integrity, and clarity. Don't deny your longing for a life that feels meaningful and authentic. Accept your desire for safety by practicing methods for grounding your energy, and learn ways to create healthy boundaries with other people. Give yourself the gift of an energetically clear environment. When your Metal qi is flowing, life will come into balance, and you can encounter new possibilities beyond your wildest dreams.

Part III

LOOKING
WITH LOVE

> "I would like to
> be shaped by the risks
> I've taken. I know that's
> going to include wrinkles, and I
> hope that the way one appears to
> others is shaped by all of the edges
> you have come to in your life, and,
> most of all, by the other faces you
> have looked into with love."
>
> — LOUISE ERDRICH

Chapter 15

━━━━◀▐▶━━━◀▐▶━━━◀▐▶━━━◀▐▶━━━◀▐▶━━━◀▐▶━━━◀▐▶━━━

TWO FACES

If you could divide anyone's face vertically and look at each half separately, you'd probably observe two very different images. You may have seen "trick" photos that make this really obvious by taking a face and putting both left sides together and both right sides together, making each composite appear very bizarre. In fact, each half of your face reveals different information: The right side is the "public" one, the image you're allowing the world to see; the left is the "private" side, where you hold your inner feelings.

The right part of your face is governed by the left side of your brain—the more logical, linear half—and emotions aren't its realm. Because it's mostly feelings that mark your face, your right side may tend to show fewer markings. The type of wrinkles you'll see on both sides of your face are "joy lines," or what are sometimes called "crow's feet" in the West. This is because they're mostly caused by smiles and laughter, and the left side of your brain is involved with humor, which is often a more intellectual exercise. In most other cases, you'll usually see more or deeper wrinkles on the left.

The left side of your face is governed by the right half of your brain, which has to do with your feeling nature. Therefore, this is where your deepest experiences are marked, where your suffering tends to be shown more strongly, and where the emotional patterns that repeat themselves may be revealed more fully. You may see sorrow lines on your left cheek, or even grief lines that are much longer. As I mentioned earlier, this doesn't indicate a negative personal quality; it simply means that you've had sorrow in your life that has influenced you deeply.

So the right side is what you're showing the world, the parts of your personality you allow others to see, while the left reveals your deeper emotions and the parts of yourself you wish to keep private. Studies have shown that most of us look more at the right side of others' faces when speaking to them, which means that we're mainly unaware of some important aspects of their private nature.

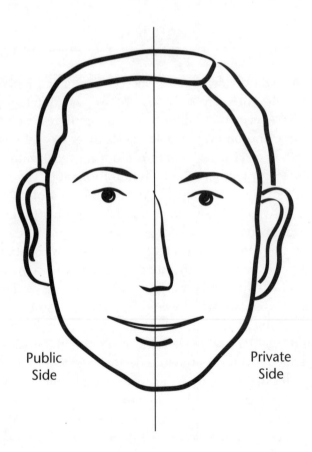

Public
Side

Private
Side

Fig. 115: The right side of your face is the public side; the left is the private side.

You can discern many things about a person when you compare one half of his face to the other. President George W. Bush, for instance, has a mouth that curls up pleasantly on the right when he speaks; but it simultaneously turns down on the left, probably revealing his level of stress, if not his true feelings about a situation.

Comparing the eyes and the areas around them can be important as well. For instance, it's not uncommon to see someone whose right eye is held larger or more open than his left. This is an indication that he may seem to be open to what you're saying, but privately, he's scrutinizing you more than he's willing to admit. It can also show that he isn't as available in relationships as he might seem on the surface. I see these kinds of eyes in many actors and others who live in the limelight, which is an example of where it's appropriate. To get people to like them, professional performers need to appear approachable; but because they're living such public lives, they need to protect their private selves as much as possible. You'll see this in how much smaller the left eye looks compared to the right.

If your left eye is held wider than your right (Fig. 116), however, it means that you're more open to others than they may initially realize. It can also mean that you're privately reading more information about them than you're letting on.

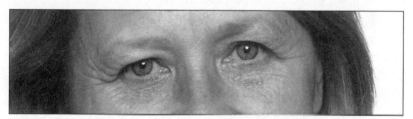

Fig. 116: When the left eye is wider, it reveals that someone is noticing more than you may realize.

You can also look for any differences in the shape of each eyebrow. If the left one is arched in an upside-down V, but the right is more curved, you may be someone who seems easygoing; but in fact, you may privately be more reactive and impulsive. You might leap into action without considering the consequences, or you may

have rapid-fire emotional reactions, but you also have a hidden ability to be spontaneous and not miss an opportunity.

The next time you're talking to someone, try looking at each side of the face separately and see if you get different views of who you're talking to! You may even find, as I often do, that it feels intrusive to look at the left side for very long.

I heard a poignant story from a student who'd developed Bell's palsy 15 years earlier. This condition occurs when part or all of the muscles of the face "freeze" and are paralyzed temporarily, sometimes causing the face to hold an unnatural expression. It can come on very suddenly and go away just as abruptly. The cause hasn't been completely determined, nor the cure, although people usually recover use of most of the muscles—some after a few months, some after years.

At the time she was stricken, my client was going through an extremely traumatic period. Her fiancé had suddenly broken off their engagement in a devastatingly vicious betrayal, and she'd been suffering for weeks with a completely broken heart, unable to even leave the house. One morning she was brushing her hair and looking in the mirror, experiencing the depths of her pain, when she exclaimed to herself, *I refuse to have these feelings!* She told me that she watched as the left half of her face began to tingle and pulled into a smiling expression—and froze that way.

From that point on, the left side of her face looked eternally happy, so she got her wish: Her private self showed only positivity and no sign of a broken heart. Interestingly, as a result, she had to train herself to smile with the right side of her face to match the left so that she wouldn't look odd. And so she presented a very pleasant expression to the world. Ever since that time, she said, everyone she meets is so nice to her, responding to someone they think is a naturally happy person.

Chapter 16

THREE FACES

Just as the face can be divided vertically and new meanings found, it can also be split the other way. In this case, three different horizontal zones give you information about how you tend to think and make decisions.

The upper third, called the "Analytical Zone," begins at the hairline and continues to the eyebrows. The middle third, the "Practical Zone," extends from the brows to the bottom of the nose, while the lowest third, the "Intuitive Zone," goes from that point to the bottom of the chin.

In evaluating your face in this way, your task is to see if any of these zones are dominant or longer than the rest, or if any are significantly shorter than the others. For many people, these separate portions are all pretty much the same size. But for some, there may be one or two zones that are extremely long or short. If you have one very large feature, such as your forehead, it's likely that the top zone will be your dominant area.

If your Analytical Zone is especially strong, it indicates that you need to examine, ponder, evaluate, and research. In order to feel good about a decision, you'll want time to think it through. Your ability to use your mind so well is your strength, but there's a risk that you'll overdo it, getting too wound up and becoming

indecisive with anxiety about all the various possibilities and consequences.

If your Practical Zone is dominant, you value common sense most of all and like to be pragmatic. Does it save time, money, or energy? Then it's probably the right thing for you to do. You aren't a penny-pincher, but you do love to find bargains. You may, however, focus too much on being frugal and not make a decision that's more emotionally fulfilling.

If your Intuitive Zone is strongest, your instincts will serve you well. You're able to get a "gut feeling" about something that will turn out to be the right way to go. You may act before you think something through, but this usually works because your sixth sense is so strong. However, you can also be too easily swayed by your emotions and make impulsive decisions.

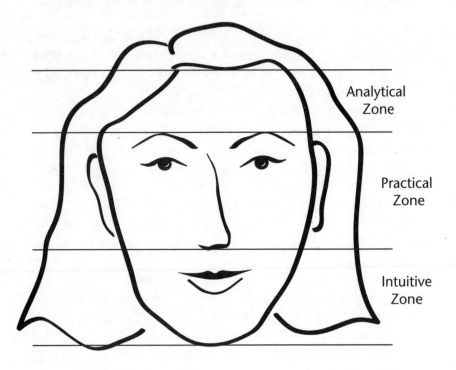

Fig. 117: The Three Horizontal Zones

So, for example, imagine that you're house hunting. If you have a strong Analytical Zone, you'll be very busy, researching the demographics of the neighborhoods you're considering, details about crime statistics, quality of schools, distance to shops, and public transportation. You'll interview several real estate agents to find the best one, scour the newspaper for listings, and analyze loan offers in detail. If your Realtor understands how to read your face, he'll know to give you as much detailed information as he can about a property and allow you plenty of time to check it out and think about it before you're comfortable with making an offer.

If you have a strong Practical Zone, however, you'll evaluate how well the floor plan will work for your specific needs, investigate the physical condition of the building, and calculate how much any repairs might cost. New plumbing or an especially efficient heating system will matter more to you than most people, and you'll consider how long you plan to live there and what the resale value might be. Your real estate agent would do best to appeal to your sensible nature and your need to have the purchase make good common sense.

If you have a strong Intuitive Zone, you may be swayed by the charming white picket fence before you even get out of the car, or it may be the antique doorknobs or the color of the master bedroom that will convince you that this is the right place. You'll be more likely to decide to buy on the spot, trusting your gut instincts—which isn't a foolish idea. Your inner sense will be correct more often than not. The agent who works with you should have all the paperwork ready to go!

What's most valuable in determining your own zones is the understanding of how you best can move forward in any situation. The point is to not fight your strengths! If you have a strong Analytical Zone, then go with that and be aware that you'll make your best decisions if you have the time and information to think about things. If your Practical Zone is dominant, you won't feel comfortable unless something makes good common sense; and if your Intuitive Zone is your strongest, then you need to trust your instincts and follow what that internal voice is telling you.

Many people have two zones that are large and one that's small in comparison. This isn't a problem; it just means that the weaker area is one that you don't need to try to use; it will be harder for you to access. In fact, it may be a relief to discover that you can let go of some old belief systems about how things "should" be done. You may have been raised by parents who drilled into you that it's essential to analyze and research, yet the lower third of your face is very long compared to your forehead. What a revelation to let go of that judgment and move into your personal decision-making power!

Chapter 17

ON FIRST SIGHT!

As you've read through the preceding chapters, it's likely that you've found something in every Element's description that you can relate to in your own personality. It's definitely true that you have some of all five in your nature, but while you can recognize their influences, there may be one that truly defines you. This will seem like your "home planet," the place and energy that feels most like who you really are and where you came from.

How do you determine what's dominant in your makeup? You observe what speaks to you most strongly when you look at your face. Check to see what features are largest or most noticeable. (You may need a friend to do this for you since, like many people, you may have a self-image that's not always realistic.) When you look at yourself, do your strongest features mostly belong to one certain Element? Are your full eyebrows the most conspicuous thing? Then you're probably living predominantly in the energy of Wood.

However, it's also quite common for people to be combinations of two Elements. In these cases, it's still possible to discern which one is your starting point. If you have a large nose and prominent cheeks, then you may "begin" in Metal. You may also have curly hair, which could mean that Fire is a second influence. With some reflection on your own temperament, it won't be difficult for you to figure out which one you start in and then where you go from there.

You might even be someone who has three or four Elements strongly represented in your face and nature. If you have a prominent chin, strong eyebrows, a full mouth, and large cheeks, for instance, you might be a combination of Water, Wood, Earth, and Metal, but lacking much of any Fire in your nature. When you read the chapter on Fire, you might have received new insights on why it's been difficult for you to relate to Fiery friends and colleagues!

Even if you're one of the rare few who has all five categories well represented in your face, there's still one that's your starting place, your home planet. If you reread the description of the personalities in Part II, you'll probably be able to discover it.

When it comes to reading other faces, I've given you so much information that it may feel daunting at this point. It might seem like there's so much to look for that you can't imagine ever being able to come to any real conclusions about who someone is! At first, many people get too caught up in the fine print—they're studiously trying to decipher the meaning of the tiniest line on their husband's cheek or the shape of his eyelids. However, you don't need to analyze someone's face in scrupulous detail. Instead, what's most important is to pull back and get the big picture.

When you first look at anyone's face, empty your mind and just observe. What one or two features are most noticeable? This will give you strong clues about what's most important to discern: which Element is emphasized in his personality. This alone will give you significant insights into who he is and why. At the very least, it will show you how to connect more easily with every person you encounter. In my work, I often don't meet my clients until the day of the consultation, but in those first few moments, face reading has given me the knowledge I need in order to establish a quick rapport with them.

Water

If the door opens and there's a Water person standing there, I immediately know that I have to make some adjustments. I don't have a lot of that Element in my nature, so I'll need to slow my Fiery tendency to talk and move quickly. I'll try to speak in more of a flow than my normal speech, and I'll focus on shifting my energy to a more fluid frequency. I won't get right down to business, but will happily wander in conversation with my client. Because she's probably more auditory in nature, my tone of voice will matter, and I'll also try to use words she can relate to: "I hear you" rather than "I see."

It's also important to be thoughtful about what I say or how I phrase things. Water may misinterpret something and her feelings will be hurt, or I might make a comment that will make her fearful. Since she'll probably keep her thoughts and reactions hidden, she won't say anything, but our personal connection may be at risk because of it.

I once had to talk on the phone with a very wealthy woman who was interested in having a large property in Europe feng-shuied. We'd been connected by a friend of mine, and I knew ahead of time that this potential client would have very little time to speak, so I made sure to be prepared with a succinct proposal for her. I didn't want to waste her time.

On the phone, I got right down to business and began to describe what I might be able to accomplish for her. But strangely, there were no sounds coming from her as there would be during a normal conversation—no "Uh-huh" or "Okay." So after a couple of minutes, I paused to wait for a question or response. There was a long silence, and then I heard, in a slow, deep tone of voice: "Whaaaat?"

Aha! I was dealing with a Water woman, so I'd been going far too quickly and had been much too direct. Fortunately, I was able to catch this in time and make the correct adjustment, starting to work "in her Element." We talked slowly, meandering back and forth in conversation about her beautiful waterfront property, dreamily exploring the possibilities of what could happen there. If

I hadn't caught the fact that she was Water, it's likely that I would have lost the opportunity to work with a lovely client.

Wood

If, however, the door opens and a Wood person is there, I have a different job. Because of this Element's tendency to be judgmental and jump to conclusions, I know that I'll need to establish my credibility with her immediately. In this case, I'll be direct and focused and get right down to business, looking straight into her eyes as I speak; and I'll concentrate on the practical aspects of my work so that it makes good common sense.

An attorney's wife once asked me to feng-shui the family house. She wanted her husband to be there for some of the consultation, and he very reluctantly agreed to humor her by spending his lunchtime at home that day. When I arrived, he'd been delayed at the office, but his gracious Metal wife and I had a lovely visit while waiting for him. Suddenly, I heard the front door slam and a briefcase hit the ground, and then a set of bushy eyebrows and a prominent jaw came through the door! Angry that he'd had to give up his free hour for this wacky feng-shui stuff, his impatience was virtually palpable.

I knew that I shouldn't start out using New Agey terms like *Energy* or *The Universe!* Instead, I immediately began to share some practical information about what their needs for the space were likely to be, based on what I was reading in their faces. This grabbed the man's attention, and it led us into a discussion of the problems he and his wife had with each other. He was fascinated and called his office at the end of the hour to cancel all his appointments for the afternoon. We spent the rest of our time together using face reading as a way of doing marriage counseling! But if I hadn't understood this man's inherent needs on first sight, most likely we would have had a polite hour together and very little would have come of it.

Fire

If the door opens and there's a Fire person standing there . . . I'm personally thrilled, because I have a lot of this Element myself! We can take off laughing and talking a mile a minute, vibrating at the same frequency. But if you don't have much in this area, you'd have to get used to how quickly this client's mind leaps to a new thought or how hard it might be for her to concentrate on what you're saying. If you're too slow, you may lose her trust or attention. You'll suddenly realize that there's no one home behind her eyes—her brain has probably gone off shopping!

Because some Fire personalities can lean toward the "drama queen" style, you may have to be prepared for a flare-up of emotion during your time together. At some point, there could be a big upset that has to do with some issue in her private life, or she might unconsciously create some chaos that intrudes on your project.

Earth

When I go to meet someone of this Element, I know that tea and cookies will soon appear! We'll share a snack, and I'll ask about the family photos on the wall or admire some special souvenir on the mantel.

Earth people's lives are usually entangled with their friends and relatives, so a lot of your conversation will include that subject. And they'll probably expect to hear something about your family, too. If you're a more solitary type or feel that this is private or an inappropriate topic of conversation, those in this Element may have a hard time relating to you. Most of all, they'll want to feel a sense of personal connection with you as soon as possible. If you haven't hugged upon first meeting, you'll definitely need to throw your arms around each other at the end of your time together!

Metal

If the person standing at the door is Metal, I don't give her a big Earthy hug! She will probably have felt me coming two blocks away and still be trying to get used to my energy. She'll notice the lint on my jacket or the speck of dirt on my shoes, and the first thing I'll need to do is show her how aware I am of subtle details. I'll also be sure to keep some distance from her when we first meet. I'll offer to take off my shoes as I enter her home and will show whatever sensitivity I can in our first few moments together. By the time we part, some Metals will be ready for a warm, wonderful hug—but some will still be relieved if I just offer my hand!

If you know ahead of time that you'll be meeting with this Element, be sure to arrive on time. In fact, reconfirming your appointment with any pertinent details a few days beforehand will be very welcome. Show that you're considerate and aware, and you will have gone a long way toward earning her trust.

Now that you've refocused on the big picture, the next chapter will help you start putting your knowledge into action. This is the most fun part: pulling it all together and reading faces!

Chapter 18

READING A FACE

After reading this book, you'll probably never look at faces in the same way again. You'll notice the ears on the FedEx delivery man, your sister's chin, and your doctor's eyebrows! And this is, in fact, the best way to integrate the information. Go play with your new knowledge and put it to use in your everyday life because that's how you'll really learn to read faces.

As an exercise in how practical this can be, you might use these tools to get out of the grocery store more quickly than anyone else—by reading the faces of the cashiers! You may have noticed that it's not always the shortest line that moves the fastest. Scan the clerks' features before you choose a line to stand in. The best advice is to avoid a Watery checker; he'll be dreamy and work in a more meandering way, which isn't great if you're in a hurry. Bypass a Fiery person; she'll be so busy flirting with the bag boy that she'll make mistakes. Don't choose an Earth clerk either, because she'll be so involved in looking at all the photos in everyone's wallets that it will take forever.

My advice is to head for the line leading to a Wood or Metal check-out clerk. The Wood guy will be organized and efficient and not interested in warm and fuzzy small talk. The Metal woman will be meticulous, and she wants you to go away from her as quickly as

231

possible anyhow! She may take a bit too long packing your groceries to perfection, but she'll always put the cans on the bottom and the eggs on top.

But of course, these principles provide much deeper opportunities when you encounter someone with whom you want to establish a long-term relationship. Figure out which Element is strong in his face and you will have discovered a trove of information. You'll identify how he'll tend to think, feel, and behave. You'll know how to speak his language and how he'll process the information. You'll be aware of what to expect from him and what he needs from you. And just as important, you won't get lost in reacting to his personality if you don't share similar Elements.

Then, if you have the opportunity, you can start to hone in on the details. His lips are full, his ears are large, his right eyebrow has a scar, his hairline is uneven, there are joy lines by his eyes, and his chin is squared. Each feature, marking, and wrinkle is a message. You're slowly getting a clear picture of who this unique being truly is.

When you first sit down with a friend or family member to practice doing a full face reading, you might not be sure where to start. After all, there's no one right way to read a face. I usually recommend remembering to relax, breathe, and smile first! Although you'll probably be referring to this book frequently in the beginning, if you keep practicing, very soon you'll discover that you're seeing so much more on your own than you ever imagined.

When I read someone's face, I don't approach her as a technician with my head full of some sort of list of things to check off. Instead, I try to empty my mind and come into the moment. The more I show up full of my own personality, the less able I am to be present and see what's there. Sometimes I begin by pulling back for a big-picture view of what the main Element is and then zoom in on the details. Other times, I start with one feature or even a marking that draws my attention more than all the others. I've learned to trust that it has some important information for me at that moment.

In general, I suggest first looking to see what feature (or features) are largest or most noticeable because doing so will usually show you which Element is this individual's home base. If she has

a large nose, it's likely that Metal will be a major aspect of who she is; if she has a strong chin, you've spotted Water as at least one of her main influences. Continue to determine if there's a second Element that is a strong factor in her nature by seeing what else is prominent in her face, and there may even be a third or fourth strong Element after that. Some people have all five Elements well represented, but you can still establish which are strongest.

If you're not sure where to go from there, you could use the facial map (see pages 42 and 43) to try reading her life story, starting with her ears and seeing if you can find any interesting experiences to ask her about from there until her present age; then look ahead into the later years to see her future potential. Move on to find any interesting wrinkles or other markings on her face and determine their meanings to add to your understanding of her life path and also her inner nature. Don't forget to observe what the two vertical sides of her face and the three horizontal zones have to tell you as well.

Remember that any specific thing you see can be showing you just one piece of information—or more than one. A marking can reveal an emotional issue she's dealing with, or it might be the sign of an important event that happened at a certain age. It may even show an aspect of her physical health. For instance, a discoloration of the under-eye area could mean that she's dealing with issues of "unshed tears," emotions that need to be released. According to the facial map, it might also be a sign that there was a life challenge in her late 30s, or perhaps it reflects some problem with the health of her kidneys. And the truth could be two of these explanations, or even all of them at once. What began with a stressful event in her 30s could be connected to her current unshed tears, and any emotional issue that continues over time can eventually develop into a physical imbalance, too.

Following are some sample faces for you to practice on. Try to read some information from each one before you go to the commentary and see what you can discover!

Fig. 118

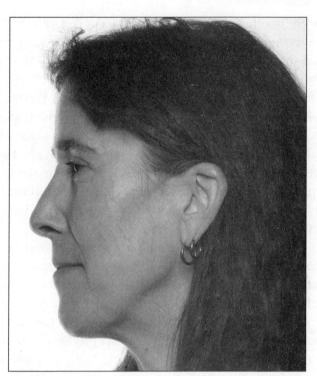

Fig. 119

One of the first things that strikes you as you look at this woman's face (Figs. 118 and 119) is her excellent eyebrows, a sign of Wood's strong drive and confidence. She'll have this Element's focused vision and the ability to work and "do." She'll probably struggle with issues of impatience, frustration, or even anger and doesn't like to be restrained from pushing forward toward her goal. In her career and in life overall, she'll enjoy developing logical systems, structure, or organization.

Her indented temples also indicate Wood's potential for compulsive behavior, difficulties with impulse control, and even addictive tendencies. The scarcity of wrinkles on her face is another indication of this Element, which keeps moving forward and doesn't hold on to old emotions as much as some others. The jaw, the last major Wood feature, is there, but not as highly defined as it could be; and it's a little narrow. This means she isn't as judgmental as some Wood people are, and may even be a bit indecisive or easily

influenced by others when trying to make a decision. Her face is a long rectangular shape, another sign of the Element; and her stature is the tall, tree kind of body type. So overall, this woman "starts" in Wood and all that this implies.

There are other Elements that show up after Wood. One is Metal—her cheeks, although not extremely prominent, are strong enough to show that she can handle authority. Her slight widow's-peak hairline reveals that she does have some Water, and the beautiful light in her eyes indicates a good supply of Fire. Her eyes also slant up, a minor Fire sign that shows optimism and curiosity. She also has some nice Earth moneybags on either side of her mouth, revealing natural reserves of energy.

The length of the middle and lower sections of her face show that her strengths lie in her good common sense combined with a remarkable level of intuitive ability. Her forehead is comparatively short, meaning that she doesn't need to analyze and research everything in order to feel comfortable. Her left eye is held a bit more narrowed than the right, meaning that she privately evaluates any person or situation more than she lets on. She isn't quite as open as she appears on the surface.

The change in the rim of her left ear indicates that she encountered challenges around the age of eight; in addition, her uneven hairline shows a difficult adolescence. The slight mark between her eyebrows could be an indication of a break with the past as she turned 40. It might also reflect some issue around bringing money or energy into her life, or it might show a slight digestive health issue—this would be determined by questioning her.

Her mouth carries some tension; her lips are a bit thin and there are some slight markings around them, which shows some Earth deficiency. This can relate to issues dating all the way back to her original relationship with her mother or issues of safety in childhood. It might translate into a lifelong feeling of being unsafe in some way and/or personal challenges with intimate relationships.

Her chin has some subtle markings on it that lead me to believe she's had to use up quite a bit of Watery willpower in her life.

Fig. 120

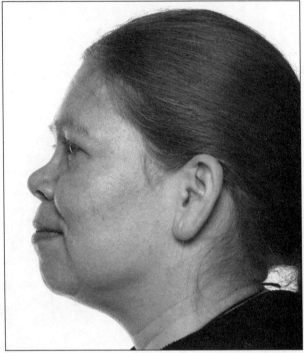

Fig. 121

This woman is half Asian and half Northern European (Figs. 120 and 121). It's important to consider racial background when reading faces; as discussed earlier, you should compare Asian faces to Asians, Caucasian faces to Caucasians, and African faces to Africans. In the case of a mixed-race person, it's necessary to consider the impact of both contributors on individual features. Asian and African faces, for instance, often have wider noses and fuller lips than those of Caucasians, and that's true here. If she were only Caucasian, we'd consider the fullness of her nose and lips to be more significant than we do in this case.

This woman is a beautiful mixture of Water and Earth. Her widow's-peak hairline, wide philtrum, and large ears and earlobes—and the overall softness of her features—show her inherent Water wisdom and creativity. She has the quiet depth that other Elements lack, and probably a strong need to express her creativity in life. If her career doesn't give her that opportunity, then she'll surely develop a hobby or even parallel profession that gives her a creative outlet. She may struggle with the common Water challenge of not being able to speak up about what she needs or what's bothering her in any situation.

Her full lower cheeks and mouth make Earth the second Element that's emphasized in her personality, and her upturned nose also shows her Earth sentimentality. These features will diminish some of her Water desire for independence; this influence will make her more likely to stay with a job, for instance, because of the need for stability and community. She may still love to travel but will have a solid home base to come back to. While she may feel the Water need for privacy and solitude, her Earth is strong enough that plentiful friendships will be important, too.

The length of her eyebrows also shows that she possesses the Wood ability to have many relationships active in her life, rather than just one or two close friends. But the fact that her eyebrows aren't full reveals a lack of confidence or assertiveness.

The area above her upper lip has some minor wrinkles developing. There's a need to evaluate how she may feel disappointed or emotionally undernourished in her life and what she might do to correct that.

While her nostrils reveal that she can spend money more freely than most people, this isn't a worry. Looking at her beautiful earlobes, we see that one of her great strengths is her gift for long-term financial planning, and the moneybags in her lower cheeks are another wonderful indication that she'll be secure in life. So while she can spend a lot, she'll also be wise about her savings and investments and balance the implications of each expenditure.

The two sides of her face are rather different. If you cover the right side to look only at the left, you will see the private sadness there, while the right side glows with her warm caring nature that welcomes you in as a true friend. Split into three zones horizontally, her face shows that her Intuitive Zone is very strong, adding even more to her already intuitive Watery nature.

Fig. 122

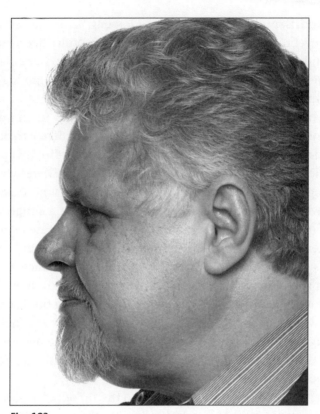

Fig. 123

Here we see a man (Figs. 122 and 123) with thick, wavy hair; a high, domed forehead; shadowing around the eyes; and a strong chin—all signs of Water. He may have the usual Elemental attributes of a highly creative personality, depth of feeling, and a life-long need for independence. His strong chin lets us know this is someone with a powerful will, even stubbornness. When combined with a slightly squared hairline, which indicates rebelliousness, this shows someone who isn't likely to just do what he's told!

After Water, the roundness in his face and his full lips and large mouth show that his energy goes to Earth next. His nose also shows some of that Element in the roundness of the tip. Relationships are important to him; he may be more openly friendly than other Water people. The Fiery joy lines around his eyes and his dimples also confirm this temperament.

Wood is probably his weakest Element, as he doesn't have strong eyebrows. This may lessen his level of confidence, assertiveness, and drive, which can be difficult for a man in our culture.

One noticeable feature is how deeply set his eyes are, signaling that while he may be friendly and kind, he might not be able to easily communicate his more private feelings, even in an intimate relationship. This, combined with his Watery tendency to be quiet or hidden, may really be important in understanding his personality. He may be much less likely to speak up or share what he's thinking. He'll play his cards close to the vest, and you could never know what he's really feeling about you or about a situation. His Earthy qualities, therefore, might be modified by these features.

Interestingly, this may be counteracted a bit by the information we get when we look at the two different sides of his face. His right eye, on the more public side, actually appears narrower, while the left is more open. So while the message he's giving out is that he's not so willing to share who he is, he's actually more available than you might think. This may be a sign of a masculine need to come across as strong and objective, thinking that his desire for connection should be hidden.

Even though there's a roundness to the tip of his nose, it's also a little pointed—a bit of Fire, indicating his curiosity and interest in how things work. There's a horizontal line across the bridge of his nose, possibly a sign of a life change around the age of 40 or else some physical issues to do with his digestive system. Last, there are subtle diagonal lines on either side of his forehead, which can be an indication of someone who has gone through some form of a "dark night of the soul" and has done substantial work in personal and spiritual growth.

Reading Children's Faces

You can read information in children's faces from the moment of birth and continue to perceive new things about them as their faces change throughout their formative years. The Chinese say that until the age of 25, a child has his "mother's face"—that is, he's still evolving through the influence of his parents until adulthood. But even though this may be true, you can see a great deal in these small faces that's theirs and theirs alone. It can be such fun to gaze at a tiny face and already see an artistic nature reflected in a rounded forehead, a curious mind represented by a pointy nose, or a little performer mirrored in a cleft chin!

Most parents feel worried about what they'll see on the ears, because this is where they'd discover any upcoming stress. It's natural to be concerned that a marking on this feature indicates a major problem at such an early age; and as a mother myself, I understand the weight of worry and the strong desire to protect kids from any harm. It's essential to remember that even if you do see something unusual on the ear, it doesn't mean the child is going to have some terrible experience; all it signifies is that there will be a challenge around the age indicated at that spot.

Remember that it's not what has happened to you that causes stress; it's how you feel about it. I often see a mark on someone's ear that matches up with the year they changed schools or a sibling was born. These kinds of experiences are part of a normal life, but they can still be difficult to deal with at the time. It's actually a wonderful benefit to be able to anticipate that some form of stress is coming for your child, because then you can plan to be available with extra support as that time approaches.

You won't find wrinkles to read in most youngsters, of course, but occasionally, as a child nears adolescence or is further into her teenage years, you may spot a line or two. For example, it's not all that unusual to see a forehead wrinkle develop at this stage, which means that there's something in her current patterns of thought or emotion—her way of perceiving the world—that's creating an opportunity for stress or a life lesson in her 20s (the decade marked on the forehead). If you can convince your child to try wearing adhesive tape on the wrinkle for a few hours, she might have some interesting revelations! As I described earlier, each time she feels the tape pull, she should pause and tune in to what she's feeling and thinking in that moment. She may well discover a pattern of similar thoughts and emotions that are creating the line and that may be contributing to some life challenge coming in her 20s.

Fig. 124

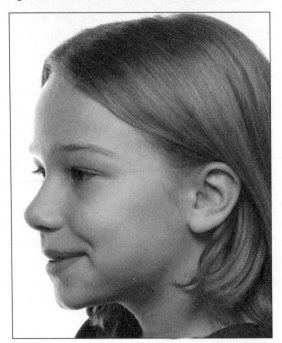

Fig. 125

This beautiful young girl (Figs. 124 and 125) has some lovely Fire in her face, most easily seen in the pointed tips of her mouth, the slight cleft in her chin (most visible in her profile), and the light in her eyes. So she'll be an exuberant child, easily excited, always in motion, and full of giggles and fun. She may experience some of this Element's anxiety or even have trouble concentrating in school due to a Fiery short attention span.

But her cheeks show a considerable supply of Metal as well, which can mean that she's a highly sensitive girl who also needs to tell others what she wants! A Metal–Fire combination can be challenging, because it only increases the likelihood that she's strongly influenced by the subtle energy of other people and her environment. But she can also be highly aware of others' needs and feelings, and the rounded inner canthus of her eyes shows her extra supply of tact and kindness in communications. Her full lips add even more Earthy qualities, meaning that she'll value friends and relationships.

Her squared chin gives her a good supply of common sense, and its strength reveals her willpower. Her eyebrows also show that she isn't so concerned about pleasing others that she won't think something through for herself. Her well-defined jaw is a sign of a Wood's strong belief system; this is definitely a girl who won't be easily swayed by others' opinions. Her excellent philtrum and slightly rounded upper forehead add a strong dose of Water—a very creative spirit!

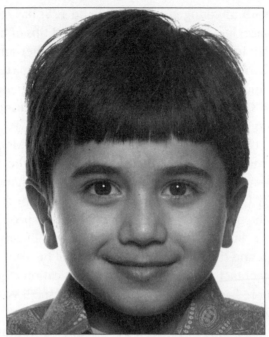

Fig. 126

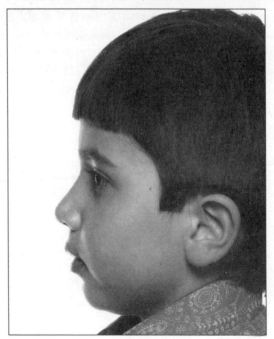

Fig. 127

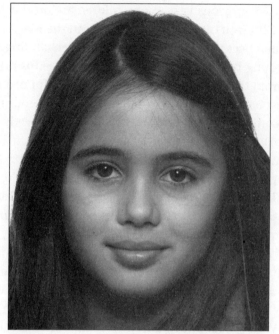

Fig. 128

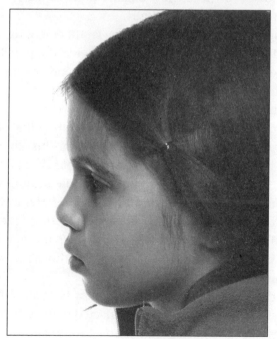

Fig. 129

These two gorgeous East Asian children are brother and sister (Figs. 126–129). You can see the similarities in their faces, but there are also differences that are important in understanding who they are. This young boy "starts" in Fire—you can see his bright spirit sparkling from those eyes! His chin also has the hint of a Fiery cleft in it. His eyebrows are strong, supplying a good amount of Wood drive and confidence; and his lower eyelids aren't overly rounded, showing his ability to evaluate a person or problem with logic rather than being too swayed by emotions.

His upper lip is thinner than his lower, which isn't unusual for males. He'll love to be pampered—by his mother at this stage in life, and later on, his partner. He has Earthy moneybags in his lower cheeks, which, along with the wide bridge of his nose, give him reserves of energy and an extra supply of caring Earth kindness.

His ears are placed rather low on his head, showing that he may find his real success in life later rather than sooner. He has full, fleshy earlobes that indicate a focus on long-term planning and extra Water wisdom overall. Because his earlobes can separate from the side of his head, he'll be able to leave the nest and not need to stay so connected to family.

Although the final form of his nose is still emerging and won't be finished until he's past adolescence, there's the possibility that it will have a bit of a point, indicating a curious nature, wanting to find out how the world works in many ways.

His sister, on the other hand, has more Water in her face than her brother. She carries a quieter Watery soulfulness that adds depth to her presence. Her eyebrows are longer than his, showing that friendships are more important to her—she has the ability to have many connections and the Wood qi to handle dealing with their various personalities, more so than her brother. Her lower eyelids are more rounded, revealing her concern for others' feelings. Her lips are fuller, again showing a person who's more emotionally expressive overall and someone for whom relationships will always be important.

Her earlobes, although mostly hidden by her hair, still let us see another trait. They're much more connected to the side of her head than her brother's, meaning that connection to family will always be more important to her. Her nose has a slight upturn, indicating a potential for sentimentality, although we won't know how much until a bit later in life, when the feature is completely formed. Her chin is a little more squared than his, revealing a sensible nature, a nice control to the soft receptivity shown on the rest of her face.

Reading all of this information can be very exciting, but just as stress comes from our interpretation of events, the effectiveness of face reading lies in how you apply it. The next chapter explores how to use your new skill to ease your journey—and that of others.

Chapter 19

EYES OF COMPASSION

I used to have two neighbors who had some problems with their relationship. One woman was very Metal, highly sensitive. A new neighbor with quite a big Earth personality moved into the house next door; she'd just been through a divorce and was coping with feelings of anger and loss. The sensitive woman soon felt the waves of strong energy emanating from this new arrival. It was too much for her to take, and she began to feel anxious and upset just by this woman's presence. She'd get twitchy when the neighbor planted flowers too close to her fence or placed her garbage cans near the property line.

The Earth person, for her part, was frustrated with this uptight woman. At first she tried to fix things by doing favors such as pulling weeds in the Metal woman's yard or bringing her newspaper to the door, but the longtime resident saw this as a boundary violation and became even more upset. It got to the point where they wouldn't come out of their houses at the same time—but even this wasn't enough to help the Metal woman feel better. She told me that she could feel the strong emotional energy through the walls, even when they were both still inside.

The new neighbor also confided in me and said, "I don't know why she's so upset. I just sit in my house and keep sending her love." While I'm sure her motivation was completely sincere, what

started out as a caring intention had to travel through all the layers of her strong, Earthy personality before arriving next door. What finally landed in the neighboring space was tinged with her energy, and of course then passed through the Metal woman's own layers of interpretation as well. What she received in the end didn't feel like love at all!

I believe that we all have one true desire in our hearts—to have a life where we're completely loved and can love completely. We go through life trying to give and wanting to receive love; but instead our experience often misses the mark. What we send out shoots way over the head of the other person, or it goes off to the left or falls short. And even if it reaches its target, it can be so colored by the two personalities involved that it gets lost in translation. Likewise, the love someone else sends us does the same thing, so both of us feel like what we're sending is not being received, and we're not getting anything in return. We may be unaware of all the ways in which those in our lives are trying to give us love, and we all end up feeling bereft.

I see this happening in so many ways. We're all walking around immersed in our personalities, and this affects how we relate to everyone else. Our personalities are really belief systems that start out based in our natural Elements, but are soon also affected by our experiences, the reactions of others, and the ways we try to cope with all of this. For many of us, these layers of beliefs build up over time into quite a thick "story" of who we think we are and how we think the world works. This perception may or may not be valid, and it might not serve us well in the long run! When we become lost in our own personal drama, we fall out of balance, are cut off from our inherent wisdom, and feel very separate from everyone else. When we're taking everything far too personally and seriously, life is difficult in every regard. Like Michelangelo's statue (which I talked about in the Introduction to this book), the angel is trapped inside a block of marble.

But if we can find a way to clear the layers of personality to reveal the natural essence within, we can see ourselves and others in a new light. We can move beyond being stuck in our small and limited perceptions into a more spacious awareness. With

our understanding of the five Elements and face reading, we can develop what I call "eyes of compassion" for ourselves and everyone we encounter. Rather than immediately reacting or making judgments, we can more easily see and accept all those in our lives for who they are and why.

More and more people these days are waking up to the fact that it's all the layers of their personal story that are blocking their progress, and they're working hard to clear them so they can move forward in a whole new way. Once in a while, someone says to me that he's worried that learning face reading will make him even more stuck in his personality. Indeed, at first glance, it can seem as if discovering your natural energies might limit you in a narrow definition of who you are—but I've found that exactly the opposite happens.

When you can see yourself in the light of the universal ebbs and flows, the yins and yangs of all of nature, you're released from the small place you've been living in. The doors swing open, the roof blows off, and you stop taking your story so personally or all that seriously. Instead of thinking that no one else shares your feelings, you recognize them as a part of the natural and universal flow of energy. The worry that fills your mind when your husband is late for dinner is some of your Earth caring, the competitiveness you feel as you aim for a promotion is a bit of Wood drive, and the anxiety that creates shallow breathing as you prepare a report is Metal perfectionism showing up. This no longer means that you're doing something "wrong," and you're not adding to the general level of stress held in your body. You can acknowledge your emotions in a new way and let them move on.

And your daughter shouting, "Look at me!" for the 17th time is just her Fire; it doesn't mean she's purposely trying to drive you crazy as you hurry to make dinner. Your partner's rejection of a nine-to-five schedule may not be immaturity; it could be his Watery need for freedom and his Elemental attraction to an unusual lifestyle . . . and these characteristics will keep showing up over the years.

When you can recognize the underlying energy in each person's nature, you're less likely to fall into reaction or blame. With your eyes of compassion, you'll have an expansive new way to view your relationships, and different choices about where to go from

here. When you learn how to read the wisdom your face reveals, you can understand how to successfully give and receive love.

While this knowledge can transform your interactions with everyone in your life, of course it's most valuable for your relationship with yourself. Finally understanding what my own face said about my innate strengths and challenges was a life-changing revelation. With my pale skin, large nose, and fine bones, I have a lot of Metal in my nature. My eyes, as well as my red hair, reveal that Fire is a strong second. As a child, I was so empathic that when I was around someone who was upset, even if they showed no outward signs of it, I'd become overwhelmed. I'd walk into an empty room and feel physically ill because of the energetic residue of emotions lingering there from an argument that had happened long ago. I was frequently sick because my system was so stressed by all the information I was soaking up from the people and places around me; I wasn't strong enough to resist most germs that floated my way.

Our experiences in childhood often define who we believe ourselves to be for the rest of our lives, but the insights that face reading provided allowed me to see myself in a new light. Instead of accepting the view that I was fragile and overly sensitive and that I needed to be very careful all the time, I could see how these early challenges had translated into my greatest strengths as an adult. The same sensitivity that made me a victim of the information around me grew into awareness and empowerment.

Learning to appreciate the nuances of Metal helped me accept and honor the ways I needed to approach life and how I could manage my energy in a positive manner. It also explained why my work expanded to encompass training others who are highly sensitive, helping them finally learn how to move through their lives in balance and strength.

Along with Fire, another strong Element in my own nature is Earth. This is why, despite my Metal sensitivity, I love to be with others. When I meet people, my first impulse is to want to help them, although this energy doesn't show up as a desire to feed them as it does in some purely Earthy personalities! Instead, it moves in combination with my Metal and Fire. I want to help by providing mental and emotional clarity, working with their subtle energy, or getting others excited about their amazing abilities.

I have a good dose of Wood Element as well, which gives me my drive and love of learning. In fact, the only weak area in my nature is Water. Knowing that this is my challenging Element helps me make healthy choices. I've learned to recognize my natural Metal tendency to deprive myself in order to make it through stressful times, but now I know that I can tap into potent Water reserves. I may be too Fiery to enjoy a long bath each night, but I've created my own ways of giving myself periods of quiet flow and deep rest in order to access the powerful wisdom this energy holds.

When you look in the mirror, try to use this knowledge to see your own story and why you've made the choices you have. For instance, how has your Water brought you courage, and when has some aspect of your Wood hindered or helped your progress? Has your Fire ever led you astray, and what can you do to rebalance? How does your Earth affect your career path? When does your Metal influence your relationships? Like me, you may discover a revolutionary new understanding of your journey and gain insights about how to travel from here.

Last, I hope that this information will bring something new to our conversations about appearance, beauty, and how our cultural beliefs make each of us feel about the way we look.

When you really understand what your wrinkles mean and how your features reflect your inner truth, why would you want to erase or change a single thing? Why would you ever choose to eliminate your purpose lines, reduce the size of your powerful nose, or even remove the mark that shows a lesson you learned from divorce or a difficult career choice? It seems to me the equivalent of throwing out your family photo album—the record of your life story! These are badges of courage, marks of honor, and signs of your inner growth and the deepening of your wisdom. Instead of thinking that you have to make your face fit the latest consensus of what superficial beauty is supposed to be, perhaps you can use this knowledge to discover, nurture, enhance, and express your true inner beauty. And when you look in the mirror, you can finally fall in love with the person you see.

AFTERWORD

Redeem, Redeem, Redeem

Inside us all is a drive to come into our own. We all feel a life-long call to be the fullest expression of the divine light found in every living thing, and we're born with our original spirit shining through. But the pure spontaneity of our beautiful essence is soon affected by our experiences in the world. In order to cope, we try to change, resist, deny, or limit who we truly are. And after a while, we lose much of the real sense of ourselves. We feel our authenticity trying to come through, but we judge it as being wrong and blame ourselves for our emotions.

What began for me as a way to understand clients better has turned out to be even more valuable as a tool for self-transforma-tion. In workshops and private consultations, I see that face reading releases self-doubt, self-blame, and confusion about why you are who you are and where to go from here. I've heard more than once that the few days someone spent in a face-reading class were more valuable than all her years of therapy!

The purpose of this work is to give you a way to rediscover and reclaim your original nature, to become who you're truly designed to be. When you live in alignment with your own inner self, you radiate a loving presence. And when you can achieve that compassion for yourself, you can hold this same space for other people as well.

The wisdom your face offers can move you beyond judgment and into clarity. There's a reason for who you are, based on the same natural rhythms, patterns, and purpose that pervade all of life. It's not about finding out what's wrong—there's nothing wrong with you or anyone else. When we can see the natural essence of each spirit we encounter, there's no judgment; there's only an awareness and understanding that allows us to love them for exactly who they are.

Who are you? What is your calling? You already have everything you need to know. It's written in your face.

ACKNOWLEDGMENTS

This is the part where I have the opportunity to thank others. When I sit down to think about it, this section could end up being longer than the actual book. So many people have taught me, guided me in the right direction, had patience with me along the way, and continue to do so. And then there are all the friends and family members who put up with my single-minded fascination with this work while "normal" life lies ignored. I am the luckiest woman in the world.

Thank you to my father, Wendall, for showing me the importance of fine-tuning communications to make information easy for others to grasp; and to my mother, Phyllis, for her lightness and vitality of spirit and for showing me the world through an artist's eyes.

Deep gratitude to many Taoist and Buddhist teachers along the way who have given me the gifts of such astonishing and elegant truths. Thank you to Charles, May, and Bokmon Dong for welcoming me into your family for 15 years of deep immersion in Chinese culture. Thank you to Louise Hay, William Spear, Lorie Dechar, Lillian Bridges, Shan-Tung Hsu, and Ursula LeGuin for being especially important mentors in my journey. Thank you to Roselle Kovitz and Terah Collins for your endlessly openhearted friendship. Thank you to everyone pictured in this book; you were

so kind to lend us your faces so we could all learn. I know that for many of you it wasn't easy, and I'm very grateful.

I thank the people who have shared sometimes small, unspoken moments with me, where a glimmer of spirit-level connection has revealed the courage and power of our hearts. Most important are all of you who have allowed me the honor of exploring the sacred beauty of your faces over the years and those of you still to come.

BIBLIOGRAPHY

Allinson, Robert, ed. *Understanding the Chinese Mind: The Philosophical Roots*. Oxford: Oxford University Press, 1991.

Beinfield, Harriet, and Efrem Korngold. *Between Heaven and Earth: A Guide to Chinese Medicine*. New York, NY: Ballantine Books, 1991.

Bridges, Lillian. *Face Reading in Chinese Medicine*. St. Louis, MO: Churchill Livingstone, 2004.

Cleary, Thomas. *Practical Taoism*. Boston, MA: Shambhala Publications, 1996.

———.*The Taoist Classics*. Boston, MA: Shambhala Publications, 1990.

Connelly, Dianne. *Traditional Acupuncture: The Law of the Five Elements*. Laurel, MD: Traditional Acupuncture Institute, 1994.

Dechar, Lorie. *Five Spirits: Alchemical Acupuncture for Psychological and Spiritual Healing*. New York, NY: Lantern Books, 2006.

Dolowich, Gary. *Archetypal Acupuncture: Healing with the Five Elements*. Aptos, CA: Jade Mountain Publishing, 2003.

Elias, Jason, and Katherine Ketcham. *The Five Elements of Self-Healing*. New York, NY: Harmony Books, 1998.

Kaptchuk, Ted. *The Web That Has No Weaver: Understanding Chinese Medicine*. Chicago, IL: Congdon & Weed, 1983.

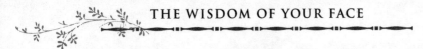

Maciocia, Giovanni. *The Practice of Chinese Medicine.* Edinburgh, Scotland: Churchill Livingstone, 1994.

Reichstein, Gail. *Wood Becomes Water.* New York, NY: Kodansha America, Inc., 1998.

Veith, Ilza, transl. *Huang Ti Nei Ching Su Wen: The Yellow Emperor's Classic of Internal Medicine.* Berkeley, CA: University of California Press, 1972.

ABOUT THE AUTHOR

Jean Haner teaches and consults internationally about powerful techniques to "read" people's inner personalities. With her 25-year background in ancient Chinese principles of balance and health, her commitment is to making this wisdom meaningful and practical for our modern lives. Her work places an emphasis on affirming ways for people to live in alignment with their own true nature and with fearless, compassionate hearts.

Jean presents workshops in Chinese face reading, from introductory to professional practitioner level, as well as corporate training and private consultations. More information is available through her Website, **www.wisdomofyourface.com**, or by calling 800-625-6307.

NOTES

NOTES

NOTES

NOTES

NOTES

NOTES

NOTES

NOTES

We hope you enjoyed this Hay House book. If you'd like to receive our online catalog featuring additional information on Hay House books and products, or if you'd like to find out more about the Hay Foundation, please contact:

Hay House, Inc., P.O. Box 5100, Carlsbad, CA 92018-5100
(760) 431-7695 or (800) 654-5126
(760) 431-6948 (fax) or (800) 650-5115 (fax)
www.hayhouse.com® • www.hayfoundation.org

———

Published in Australia by: Hay House Australia Pty. Ltd.,
18/36 Ralph St., Alexandria NSW 2015
Phone: 612-9669-4299 • *Fax:* 612-9669-4144
www.hayhouse.com.au

Published in the United Kingdom by: Hay House UK, Ltd.,
The Sixth Floor, Watson House, 54 Baker Street, London W1U 7BU
Phone: +44 (0)20 3927 7290 • *Fax:* +44 (0)20 3927 7291
www.hayhouse.co.uk

Published in India by: Hay House Publishers India,
Muskaan Complex, Plot No. 3, B-2, Vasant Kunj, New Delhi 110 070
Phone: 91-11-4176-1620 • *Fax:* 91-11-4176-1630
www.hayhouse.co.in

———

Access New Knowledge.
Anytime. Anywhere.

Learn and evolve at your own pace
with the world's leading experts.

www.hayhouseU.com